LIFE IS LIKE A PUZZLE

A picture of a puzzle held in the air
Is on the cover of this book, that we see.
The three are trying to help balance it
To illustrate that life can be like that for you and me.

Yes, life can be like a puzzle.
It's up to us to choose.
The pieces are the choices we make in life
That will help us be successful or else lose.

At times our choices might be hard.
They can be up in the air.
We may need to seek advice
From our parents, teacher, counselor, pastor:
As well as from our God in prayer.

Life can be full of meaning and purpose.
We can "shine like stars in the universe."
If we take control of our lives, we can earn a crown
And be a success and not a curse.

It's up to you and me to balance life's puzzle each day.
And we can, if we take hold of our lives in every way.
All of us have an inner spirit and a talent that's real.
That a loving God can reveal.

A Guide—
Ways to Succeed

VOLUME ONE

MARGARET A. ROSENBERGER

Inspiring Voices®
A Service of **Guideposts**

Inspiring Voices books may be ordered through booksellers or by contacting:

Inspiring Voices
1663 Liberty Drive
Bloomington, IN 47403
www.inspiringvoices.com
1-(866) 697-5313

ISBN: 978-1-4624-0276-2 (sc)
ISBN: 978-1-4624-0275-5 (e)
Library of Congress Control Number: 2012914514

Printed in the United States of America

Inspiring Voices rev. date: 09/18/2012

I have to live with myself, and so,
I want to like myself wherever I go.

CONTENTS

APPENDIX

OTHER PUBLICATIONS BY MARGARET A. ROSENBERGER

My God of Love, Mercy, Angels and Miracles
Secrets and Songs of Payne's Prairie, Volume One
My Pets and I
A Teacher's Odyssey (Secrets and Songs)
Poems for Children
My Angels and I
Spiritual Interpretations of God's Truths
The Birth and Growth of The Village - (North Florida
Retirement Village)
Secrets and Songs of Payne's Prairie, Volume Two
Secrets and Songs of Payne's Prairie,
Volume Two, Condensed Version
The Other Side Where Love Knows No Color
A Lifetime of Humor, Volume One
(Compiled with Frances B. Head)
A Guide—Ways to Succeed, Volume One
A Guide—Ways to Succeed, Volume One, Condensed Version
A Guide—Ways to Succeed - Volume Two, Comparative
Religion, Pending
A Lifetime of Humor, Volume Two
(Compiled with Frances B. Head)
The Saint Augustine Song (Sheet Music)
Correspondence Notes
Old Gainesville Scenes
Old St. Augustine Scenes
PUBLICATIONS, IF AVAILABLE
Rose Hill Publications
8015 NW 28th Place, B105
Gainesville, Florida 32606
rosehilllpublications@hotmail.com
(352)375-4816

ABOUT THE AUTHOR
by
Frances B. Head

When Margaret Rosenberger was a small child, her teacher-aunt, in conducting career days, asked her what she'd like to be when she grew up. She replied, "I'd like to work in a store or a restaurant," to which her aunt inquired, "Why would you choose those jobs?" Margaret responded, "Because I want to help people."

The author has fulfilled that wish many times over in her personal, professional and spiritual life. Spearheading the Children's Committee to "Rescue and Keep Youth from Crime" and originating **A Guide—Ways to Succeed** with many character building poems are just the latest in her history of service.

At age eleven in the small town of Micanopy, Florida, where she grew up, she taught a Sunday School class. When a pianist was needed, she undertook the responsibility. Her service to the church has continued through the years: directing the church choir, organizing a youth group and serving as Moderator for the business meetings.

Margaret's earliest schooling was in Micanopy; her high school training was at P. K. Yonge Laboratory School, now P. K. Yonge Developmental Research School. She attended Stetson University for two years and spent her last undergraduate year at the University of Florida in its first year of coeducation. Rosenberger graduated from the University of Florida with honors, earned a Masters of Education and also completed further post-graduate study.

Her thirty-two years in education, supervision and administration include: teacher, principal of three schools, general supervisor and elementary school supervisor of the district, and teacher for a year in Heidelberg, Germany, in the U. S. Army Dependents' School. The year included extensive travel in twenty-one different countries in Europe, Africa, the Near and Middle East, encompassing Germany, Greece, Crete, Turkey, Lebanon, Syria, Jordan, Egypt, Iraq, Switzerland, Austria, Netherlands, England, France, Belgium, Denmark, Sweden, Norway, Italy, Spain, Scotland and at other times, most of Canada.

Before her stint in Germany, Rosenberger was general supervisor of the Alachua County School District. Continuing her life's purpose of helping others, Rosenberger worked to obtain kindergarten for all of the "colored schools," as they were called then, and laid the groundwork for the beginning of the United Way Fund, the Media Center, the bicycle lanes and the spelling bees.

Upon her return from Germany, the author was asked to be elementary school supervisor, assisting the faculty, the principals and the newly-appointed Black elementary school supervisor in planning the activities, curriculum and the application of materials for use in the schools.

The especial motivation of Rosenberger's next project to help others—this time, the elderly—was the unkind and negative treatment given her father in a nursing home. She was a major force in organizing and helping to bring to fruition the North Florida Retirement Village, Inc.— even a last minute effort to raise additional money to meet the criteria of financial supporters, Florida National Bank and Morrison's Food Service, Inc.

Rosenberger was made an Emeritus member of Altrusa International Club of Gainesville. Her active membership continues in her church, the Delta Kappa Gamma Society, (ASCAP) American Society of Composers, Authors and Publishers, Order of the Eastern Star, NARFE (National Association for Retired Federal Employees); and Alachua County and State Retired Educators Associations.

Rosenberger has been the recipient of many honors. Recognitions include being named "Boss of the Year" in 1973. She was honored with the Alachua-Bradford County Women of Distinction Award by Santa Fe Community College (now Santa Fe College) in 2005; The Distinguished Alumna Award by the University of Florida, P. K. Yonge Developmental Research School in 2006, and Emeritus Board Member of North Florida Retirement Village, SantaFe HealthCare in 2007. She is listed in *Who's Who of American Women, Who's Who in American Education, Who's Who in Publications, Personalities of the South,* and *Royal Blue Book, Leaders of the English Speaking World.*

FOREWORD

A primary result of the "Committee to Rescue and Keep Youth from Crime" has been to remind the community of the problems of youth and potential solutions to them.

The purpose of the committee, led by Margaret Rosenberger, has been to inform, motivate and inspire the young people in understanding and applying better means whereby they can solve their problems.

Further, **A Guide—Ways to Succeed** can be the instrument by which students, parents, teachers and community leaders can discuss the poems as they apply to the principles of every day living. In addition, parent workshops, counseling and instruction would be a good resource.

The poems in the guide explain and instruct students in how to respond in different situations and to make the right choices. The problems of drugs, cheating, respect for self and others, for instance, exemplify the need for the choice of best behavior.

The public schools, for example, could possibly include the guide in the curriculum, as could home schools and spiritual leadership organizations.

If this guide is helpful, then the author's purpose will have been achieved.

— *Frances B. Head,* Editor

THOUGHTS
(For possible discussion).

Do everything in love. – 1 Corinthians 16:14 (NIV)

The quality, not the longevity, of one's life is what is important – Martin Luther King, Jr.

The supreme happiness of life is the conviction that we are loved— loved for ourselves; nay, rather, loved in spite of ourselves. – Victor Hugo

Do not let your hearts be troubled and do not be afraid. – John 14:27 (NEW)

The aftermath of violence is tragic bitterness. – Martin Luther King, Jr.

Order breeds habit. – Henry Adams

The purpose of a family is for the formation of people who are able to love. – Rosemary Haughton

Never, never, never, never give up. – Winston Churchill

If we expect mediocrity, that's what we get. – S. John Davis

For myself, success is, during this earthly pilgrimage, to leave the woodpile a little higher than I found it. – Paul Harvey

Act as if it were impossible to fail. – Dorothea Brande

Nothing is particularly hard if you divide it into small jobs. – Henry Ford

Nothing in the world can take the place of persistence. – Calvin Coolidge

The object of teaching a child is to enable him to get along without a teacher. – Elbert Hubbard

A child regards your cheery smile as an evidence that you are on his side, so he relaxes and is happier. – George W. Crane

It is the parents who allow their children to do everything they please who are not loved later on in life. – Fulton J. Sheen

Father Time lays his hand lightly on those who have used him well. – Charles Dickens

SUGGESTIONS FOR USE OF
A GUIDE —WAYS TO SUCCEED

Use the guide with an individual or in a group with one book or a book for each individual.

- Select a poem to start the day for a discussion of the subject.
- Inquire as to what is known about the subject and list answers on a board or on a sheet of paper.
- Discuss or look up unknown words or phrases in the poem that will be introduced.
- Read aloud the poem selected for discussion for the day or week.
- Ask questions; discuss and list new thoughts or ideas gleaned from the poem.
- Compare and evaluate the first list of what was known about the subject of the poem with that of the second list of what was learned after hearing or reading the poem.
- Encourage listeners or readers to write on a separate paper possible changes or corrections needed in his or her life.
- Encourage the participants to eat meals with the family; share the poem or the contents of the poem and the lessons learned.
- Encourage each individual to remain in school, get a good education and stay away from drugs, street gangs and crime.
- Discuss good care of property, books and other items belonging to self and others, especially if the book used is school property.
- Lead participants to a happy, purposeful and successful life with a recognition of self worth and respect for self and others.

APPRECIATION TO PARTICIPANTS IN THE SMALL WORKSHOP

This book was written and inspired
By work with the Alachua County Children's Committee.
If we do not recognize special people who met and worked,
Lack of that tribute would be such a pity.
"In Appreciation" is more complete in the back of the book.
Names have been listed there— their merit to inform.
Those who have attended the small group workshop,
Have been helpful in editing and making
suggestions, as we'd brainstorm.
Alvin and Mary Butler were a good part of this team.
They shared personal experiences and
suggestions they'd gleaned.
Dr. Charles Hall, representative of the
Superintendent of Schools, made it clear
That we should separate church and public
school— that we hold so dear.
Attorney Heather Jones, who works with the State Attorney,
Has read and offered legal suggestions to
lead us in this work and journey.
Capt. Tony Jones, community and youth
leader, who is currently Chief of Police,
Has attended and offered encouragement— with
hopes for progress, change and peace.
Dr. Jo Ann Parham has served as advisor and reader.
As a former missionary, teacher, and dean
of a college, she has been a leader.
The Rev. John A. Parker has attended and added his voice.
He has let it be known that he believes that
this work is on the right course.
Atkins Warren, former Chief of Police and leader in the state,
Was present and knew the problems of youth and their fate.
The last to join our workshop was Christy Cain,

From the Victim Advocate's office, and
we were so glad that she came.
Later, together with Beth Boyles, leader and
President of Retired Educators,
Dr. Fran Vandiver, Principal and Director of P. K. Yonge,
Became a part of the praises to be sung.
They, along with Rebecca Mickholtzick,
Assistant State Attorney, Juvenile Division Chief,
Helped critique the collection, after due
reflection, study and belief.
These poems have been written and studied with loving care
To help lead youth to a successful life, a wish we all share.

— *Margaret A. Rosenberger*

DEDICATION

This book is dedicated to all those who read
To find a guide for ways to succeed.
This book expresses love for all of mankind
The reader might learn from its contents and good
lessons find.

This book was written in poetic form;
Therefore, it is not in the usual norm.
It was written with loving thoughts and prayers.
It was written by one who really cares.

This book was written for those in their youth;
For those in trouble or those seeking the truth;
For parents whose love for their children is so kind;
And for those who need a guide or a change of mind

This book was written for pupils in school
Who want to learn and follow the Golden Rule★.
For teachers who seek new ideas and ways
To offer encouragement and then give praise.

This book can be used in church, mosque or temple
For those who want a guide that's pure and simple.
As the author, I hope many will be blessed,
Because it encourages others to do their very best.

★Golden Rule: The rule or principle of treating others as one wishes
to be treated.

DEAR READER

There are many after school choices
Where you can go, study or play.
Decide on a variety of activities,
And you'll learn much along the way.

There are those who will mentor or tutor
Youth who need help after school.
Try to decide on what will help the most,
But be sure you follow each policy and rule.

There are places to visit to help others;
Such as, a nursing or retirement home.
Others might need yard work,
Writing or cleaning—or help with calls on the phone.

This study will help you to get along
With other people; such as Red and Yellow, Black and White.
It will help guide and direct you
In doing what is good and right.

There are teachers, pastors and chaplains who might help
In this study along the way.
Read and discuss only one poem
And what it says to you that day.

The thoughts within this next section
Were written for me and you.
You might find it quite worthwhile to study this work
And learn better what to say and do.

TO ALL YOUNG PEOPLE
EVERYWHERE

To all young people everywhere:
Choose your close friends with the greatest of care.
Choose those who think and believe as you,
If you would be happy your whole life through.
Be kind and thoughtful in every way;
Remember others if you bow to pray;
Avoid the appearance of what looks wrong;
Be faithful and truthful, steadfast and strong.
Treat others as you would like to be treated.
Plant good seeds wherever you see they are needed;
Be a good leader and choose the best road;
Help others by lifting or lightening their load.
Help make your country strong; help build a better town;
Keep an understanding heart; share a smile rather than a frown.
Give service to your community and fellow man;
Let this be a part of your over-all plan.
Try to be a good neighbor and show respect and love,
For you can have great joy that brings peace like that from above.
Go about helping and trying to do good.
But lean on your teachings to help you do as you should.
Help rid the world of selfishness and hate:
Seek someone who is an equal to be your help-mate.
Have a reason and purpose in all that you do.
Be one who can honor, cherish and be true.
Be patient and honest as you come and go.
Take a stand for what's right; let the whole world know.
Choose carefully, young people, for tomorrow is yours.
Use this formula! It's one that assures—
And it's one that endures.

WHAT INTERESTS THE YOUTH

The youth were asked to complete a survey
So that leaders would be able to show them the way.
It is hoped that the legislators will give of their time,
And the support of foundations and benefactors will fall in line.

The most important subject to the youth
Was to learn more about good nutrition
and snacks, if you want the truth.
The second subject about which the youth wanted to learn
Was the dangers of drugs, tobacco and alcohol—a great concern.

The third item of interest was to learn about sports.
They wanted to learn the rules and
regulations on the field and courts.
The fourth highest interest was learning how to bank:
How to make deposits, write checks and
how their credit might rank.

Of course, the youth wanted to learn how to type,
Learn bookkeeping skills and learn how to write.
They would like instruction on how to build a
house and administer first aid.
They'd like to learn how to care for the sick
and how to accept counseling when they have strayed.

They'd like to learn how to care for someone who is ill—
How to bathe or walk with one and other needs to fill.
They'd like to learn to give the Heimlich maneuver and C-P-R.
They'd like to learn how to check information
on the Internet from near and far.

WHAT INTERESTS THE YOUTH
(CONTINUED)

Trades and crafts, the recreation centers should teach—
How to cook, set a table, and learning good
manners should be within reach.
The youth would like to learn ways to stay out of jail;
How to be a witness or how to go on one's bail.

They'd like to learn Spanish, how to read and speak
And learn vocational skills for a future job they might seek.
They'd like to learn parenting skills, school rules
and about the P. T. A.
And how to sew, patch and care for clothes in a special way.

The youth would like to learn art, folk and patriotic song.
They'd like to visit and study the homeless and help A. A.
members to be strong.
They'd like field trips to correction and juvenile institutions,
And learn more how religion can inspire
to make good resolutions.

Then let the educators and testers learn from the youth,
And plan the curriculum that will reach them in truth.
As we listen to our youth and what's on their mind,
Their response might mean less violence, drugs and crime.

This book, **A Guide—Ways to Succeed,** was inspired
by the results of the surveys taken by the pupils at Reichert
House, an enrichment school for youth, Gainesville, Florida, as to
which subjects interested them most and by the adult leaders and
participants on the Alachua County Children's Committee as to
the subjects they thought most beneficial to the students.

CPR - CARDIOPULMONARY RESUSCITATION
P. T. A. - PARENT TEACHER ASSOCIATION
A. A. - ALCOHOLIC ANONYMOUS

SMILE

When everything goes wrong.
And the sun no longer shines,
Just sing a little song
Or repeat some cheering lines.

When the world turns against you
And the rain comes pouring down,
You can keep from being blue
By throwing away that ugly frown.

After the rain, the sun shines bright,
And after time, you will forget
The cloudy day that was like night,
So smile! Smile! You'll ne'er regret.

WHEN YOU WERE BORN

Hopefully, when you were born,
You were a bundle of joy.
You were welcomed with open arms,
And were a ray of sunshine—whether a girl or boy.

You were nurtured and led
By a grown person, no doubt.
But you are responsible for yourself,
So don't whine, cry, rave or pout.

The world is open to you;
And it is up to you to do what is good.
So study and read good books for yourself,
And attend a spiritual establishment in your neighborhood.

When we place what is good first in our lives,
We'll follow great leaders who taught that
we should love one another.
When we do, we'll obey our laws, values, ethics, and principles,
And follow in their steps as an adopted sister or brother.

Suggestions: Ask "Who are some of your admired leaders. They could be spiritual leaders or political; they could be neighbors, friends, teachers, preachers, authors, parents, composers, etc." Then ask, "Why do you admire them?"

WHEN I WAS A CHILD

When I was a child, what wonderful mirth
To seek the many treasures that were placed here on Earth!
I walked in the woods and watched the sunset.
The flowers I picked, I'll never forget.

When I was a child, I spoke my own tongue,★
As I laughed and sang with the very young.
I walked by the sea and God seemed so near.
He seemed to hold my hand and said, "Do not fear."

Back then, I was humble, forgiving and kind,
Believing and trusting with an open mind.
Though I've learned some ways of humankind,
Childlike I still hunt for the good things I'll find.

When I was a child, harder I would try
When challenged by others more competent than I.
Though I am grown now, may others see
Many joys of my childhood still living in me.

★Tongue – meaning speech, language, dialect, and vocabulary.

(With minor revisions, the above poem was published in *Secrets and Songs of Payne's Prairie* by Margaret A. Rosenberger, Copyright 1998).

YOU ARE AN INDIVIDUAL

You are an individual who needs recognition.
You want to be known for what you are.
Seize each opportunity to excel,
Then you'll have a special name and can be a star.

You are important, so respond to encouragement.
Belittling remarks can hurt your pride.
It is cruel to hear harsh and unkind words,
So, listen, weigh them, and then lay them aside.

It is important that you have good self-esteem,
So develop your talents to a high degree.
Cultivate friendships that are good for you,
Share your time with others, and be the best you can be.

AFTER ADDICTION TAKES ITS TOLL

Here I am looking like a bum;
I'm high on drugs and am having fun.
I know the mixes and the fixes,
But when I see the police, I'm on the run.

My car is packed with paraphernalia.
I have marijuana under my car seat.
When I go to—you won't know where—
Some good buddies, I plan to meet.

My supplier is a friend of mine.
Illegal drugs, he wants me to sell.
I'll never tell anyone from whom I buy
Or believe my path is the way to Hell.

I don't need God or religion, for goodness sake,
No one can tell me anything I don't know.
When I am high, I'm on "cloud nine"
And I expect to make a lot of dough.

Don't tell me; I don't need a sermon.
Just leave me alone, and happy I'll be.
After all, I know my way around.
I'll soon be twenty-one, and I'm responsible for me.

KNOW AND APPRECIATE YOUR SURROUNDINGS

I believe there's good in most everything,
And if we look around, we will see
The beauty that surrounds us
Was placed here for you and me.

Many of us are made to emulate our father and mother.
Traits were pre-determined before we were born.
Our parents' expectation and joy were great
On that evening or on that special morn.

We all come from different backgrounds.
No one has the same stature or face.
But everyone has red blood within,
No matter what the country, city, faith or race.

Since we were all designed and in an image like no other,
We should use our uniqueness to do our very best.
When we serve our God, our home, school and country,
We will want to help others.
The good or bad that we do will be known in life's final test.

Then enjoy who you are and the beauty that surrounds you.
Smell and admire the flowers while you may.
Tell your parents and others that you love them.
You'll be glad that you did, once you've had your say.

LOOKING FOR WORK?

The poem below is a true story written about a pupil in fourth grade who came seeking counsel with me, his principal. It was inspired by and written after attending a meeting to "Rescue and Keep Youth from Crime." Perhaps it can be used as a lesson for career discussion and for possible study in vocabulary building, reading, spelling, writing, and legal ethics to help youth in choosing and following a good path.

I once had a young boy in school.
He was not sure about the policies that rule.
He came to me one day and said
He wanted to do what was right, and so he pled.

"My family is poor, though both parents work.
I want to help out at home, but my school work not to shirk.
Now a strange man came along and offered me a deal,
But I'm not sure about it; it's doubt that I feel."

"He said, I could make <u>lots</u> of money in no time,
But it seems to me, I might commit a crime.
As my principal, I trust you in what you have to say,
And I'd like for you to guide me so I do not go astray."

When he told me that drugs were what he would have to sell,
Much counsel and advice to him were important to tell.
"Illegal drugs are not good for body or soul.
They may give you a high, but some cause
depression, or death takes its toll."

LOOKING FOR WORK (CONTINUED)

"It is illegal to sell drugs and commit a crime.
You'd be separated from family and friends,
because you'd have to do time.
Juvenile detention is no place you'd want to be;
And as you get older, you could end up
in the Federal penitentiary."

"If you want to make money, find a job that people need.
Sweep sidewalks, mow yards, or to blind people read.
Learn first aid and sit with ones who are ill.
There are many good areas of work that you can fulfill."

"On a farm there are always chores to be done.
Working with plants and animals could be fun.
There are other jobs to which you can aspire.
With good work habits you may qualify for hire."

"Managers in stores always need people to shelve their stock.
Placing products on shelves is better than ICE, or a high on rock.
Be above reproach in all things and do not steal.
You'll be glad later, because you refused the drug deal."

"Whatever you do, in school please stay.
Work hard; do right and accept only legal work each day.
In every endeavor do the very best that you can.
In that way, you'll help, not hurt, your fellow man."

"On weekends, a place of worship try to find.
A good message and hymns can be a balm to your mind.
Ministers and teachers of spiritual institutions
can provide a good day
As they steer and guide you in a wholesome and good kind of way."

LOOKING FOR WORK (CONTINUED)

"I don't ever want to see you or your name on TV or in the news
For selling marijuana, drugs or making homemade Booze.
Find the kind of work that you really enjoy.
Value your own life and that of others— "DO NOT DESTROY."

"Be clean and neat in your speech and attire.
Your being a good and productive citizen is what I desire.
When you are punctual, faithful and truthful in all that you do,
You'll find that respect, acceptance and success will come to you."

Others are watching you.

A VISIT TO THE PRINCIPAL BY A FIFTH GRADER

"A well-dressed man approached me,
And said a lot of money I could make.
I would need to sell drugs at home and school.
He said it would be as easy as eating a piece of cake.

"As my principal, what do you think I should do?
I need to make money to help with food and school.
As a young child would it be illegal?
Should I agree to sell drugs, or would it break a law or rule?"

"As your principal, first, I would tell your parents.
Then I would go with them to the police on his beat.
That man needs to be taken off of the street;
So he can't entice others, because addiction leads to defeat.

"Now if you need to make money,
I know someone who needs you now.
It would require you to sweep her roof and walk
Or help her with her chickens and a cow.

"Anyone who is honest and kind
And wants to make for himself a good life
Will stay in school and work hard
And say "NO" to selling drugs that would lead to jail and strife."

The illustration in the above poem actually took place. The fifth grader involved went to work, with the permission of the child's mother, to sweep the roof and walk and then did some other work for a senior citizen.

CHOOSE YOUR FRIENDS WISELY

When you are choosing your friends,
Be sure that you make a good selection.
If you don't choose your friends wisely,
You could lose your good reputation and face rejection.
People would not listen to what you say.
When they see you are on the wrong tracks.
They would look at you with suspicion,
They would question your motives and acts.
Even your family members might not trust you—
Although at times they might try.
Many will question you, even though the truth is said,
Because you have become known to lie.
To have friends one must be friendly.
This is an obvious fact most say.
Choose ones who'll not get you into trouble,
Because they have chosen the wrong way.
Seek friends who are kind and sincere—
Those who care for you and will cause you no fear.
If there are problems, they'll help bring relief,
And they'll stand by you in joy or in grief.
Find friends who obey and keep the laws.
They will not have to explain the "why" or "because."
True friends will lift you up when you are down
And bring you smiles instead of a frown.
Then please select your friends and companions wisely.
The best are those who would never say fail.
Bad friends will corrupt your life,
But good friends will lead and help you stay out of jail.

DISCIPLINE

No one said life would be easy,
Cause it's full of pain as well as joy.
With sound discipline you can solve some problems
With any diligent means you might employ.

You must confront your problems
In order to resolve all of them.
Those things that hurt, often instruct,
But in the process, you can become like a polished gem.

You must learn to delay gratification;
Begin your chores and don't delay.
Learn to accept responsibility;
Not postponing each task is the best way.

You are a valuable person—
The cornerstone of self-discipline and self-worth.
The love of your parents gives great assurance
With their devotion to you since birth.

Hopefully, your parents teach self-discipline and self-restraint,
As well as good morals and how to live.
They are role models as they demonstrate in love:
Obedience and treatment of others is the best advice they can give.

You have all the time there is.
It is up to you as to how your time is used.
Refrain from skipping classes or school.
Be free from fights and drugs, so that your life you have not abused.

Do that which is most difficult first.
Do your homework before watching TV.
By doing that which is most important or difficult first,
You and your time can be as productive as they should be.

DISCIPLINE (CONTINUED)

There are some things you cannot change,
But usually you do have the freedom to choose.
Then live each day doing the best that you can.
In time, success will come and you'll surely win, not lose.

Be a winner!

FACTS ABOUT CHEATING

Headlines voice concerns in the daily news:
Relate how pupils readily cheat,
And that it's acceptable among students and parents
Who think it's a cool way to compete.

Teachers and leaders have been silent
About the trend in and out of school.
But if someone doesn't speak up about the issue,
We might as well abandon each rule.

Possibly some of the problems may go back to the parents,
Because cheating on each other has been the game.
They have neglected their values and morals
And each one has refused to accept the blame.

With divorce, the children are full of frustration,
Because of heartbreak, they weep bitter tears.
It is all because a parent cheated
And brought about a life of separation and fears.

As a teacher and principal, I believed that most pupils are honest—
At least most of the time when backed by parents as support.
Although I have seen those who cheated on tests—
Even signed the names of their parents on a report.

When pupils are counseled to understand
That the best achievers do not cheat;
They should avoid making a bad name for themselves:
Learn from their mistakes—not to repeat.

FACTS ABOUT CHEATING
(CONTINUED)

They don't want to go to a doctor
Who cheated in his work.
They don't want to go to banker
Who steals his money or his other duties shirk.

As a reminder to students, I'd like to say,
"I hope you'll choose an above reproach lifestyle
In which you can live, work and play.
Even though others may cheat,
You have to decide what you are going to do;
But since you have to live with yourself,
Try to be responsible, faithful and honest,
And good things should come back to you."

Do your own work and do your best.

WE LEARN BY EXAMPLE

As children, we learn by example.
Being more concerned about clothes, a home, a car, a bike, or money,
We disregard the needs and thoughts of others.
Material things are not as important as a life that's happy and sunny.

Although we may not always agree
With our parents or an elder adult,
There are school and religious personnel with whom we can confer.
They will be glad to give time to counsel or consult.

When we have concern for each other,
We are unselfish and forgiving with a loving way.
We can find Love in the affectionate eyes of our parents,
And even hold hands when we come together to pray.

We need the love and attention of both parents.
Our fathers should spend time with us each day.
Neither parent can take the place of the other.
Economics is not as important as parents' leading the way.

Regular church or other religious attendance is important;
Fellowship with others of like mind and belief is best,
Because they strengthen one's good qualities
That measure up to a final test.

TEMPER TANTRUMS

Temper tantrums are a part of being a child.
As you mature, these traits can be outgrown.
You can find opportunities for growth on a level of being an adult.
Maturity can come with age, and that is well known.

Minds and bodies seem to develop about the same rate.
After twenty-one, many youth can reason well.
They can relate facts and solve problems,
And with older adults, they can serve and current events tell.

Now, if you have temper tantrums,
You lack discipline and are immature.
It is hard for you to accept responsibility
And in making decisions, you are un-sure.

You need help in selecting your clothes.
Handling money doesn't seem a care.
You have not learned how to plan for the future,
The idea of working and supporting
yourself is not a serious affair.

You have not yet learned to admit mistakes
Or recognize it when things are not right.
You still feel you've been abused and sulk
Instead of knowing and doing what is upright.

TEMPER TANTRUMS (CONTINUED)

Why not try to think before you act?
If necessary, count up to ten.
Perhaps maturity will gradually increase.
And with patience you'll face the world and win.

Look yourself in the mirror,
And ask yourself, "What should I do?"
With patience and hard work, you will choose the good life,
And good things will come back to you.

HEALTH AND HYGIENE

Not only is it important
That you eat right each day;
But you should take care of your body
In a careful and thorough way.
Take a daily bath: morning and/or night,
So bacteria on your body won't grow.
Use a deodorant under your arms;
This is good advice that you should know.
At least once a week, shampoo your hair.
If it's neat and clean, others realize you care.
If possible, visit a dentist twice a year.
Brush your teeth up and down.
Use a floss between your teeth
To avoid decays, thus keeping them sound.
It's good to use a mouth wash
To keep your breath clean and sweet.
This also helps make your mouth bacteria free,
And you avoid offending those you greet.
Get some exercise out-of-doors,
And keep up with your homework and your chores.
In your desire to gain respect,
Be neat and clean wherever you go.
Your good and honest work, others will come to know.
Then make for yourself a worthy name;
It could lead to a path of wealth and fame.

WHEN YOU ARE TEMPTED

When you are tempted to use or sell drugs,
Let your answer be the same.
"Don't ask me! No, not me!
I'm not in that illegal game."

"I don't want to go to prison
Where no one can go my bail.
I don't want to be separated from friends and family
And spend a long time in jail."

There are consequences for illegal acts.
Of this you may be sure.
So find a good purpose for your life
Where peace, love, and happiness will endure.

SIX CHOICES OF ALLEGIANCE

Avoid going down that slippery slope.
Hold on to your morals and values; stay off of dope.

Be faithful to your God in what you do,
And be loyal and patriotic to your country too.

Your family should be included to whom you are true;
Forsake them not in old age as some people do.

Your next choice should be to your club or school,
Where you know and follow each policy and rule.

Your very good friends should be faithful and kind;.
They are precious and rare and hard to find.

Yes, stay off of that slippery slope:
Hold to the path of integrity and its hope.

In making decisions, ask yourself would this choice please:
1. - My God?
2. - My Country?
3. My Family?
4. My Club or School?
5. My Friends?
6. Yourself?

If the answers are "Yes" to most of these questions, then the
decision would probably be the right one for you.

IF YOU ARE ASKED TO
JOIN A GANG

If you are asked to join a gang,
And spend late hours on the street,
Ask yourself, "Why should I do that?"
It could lead to stealing or killing and tragic defeat."

Tell the one who asks,
"I need to be in bed to get my sleep.
In that way, I'll avoid trouble
That might make my friends and family weep."

BE CAREFUL OF WHAT YOU
SERVE OR DRINK

Do not serve or drink alcoholic beverages.
It is best that you abstain.
After you are twenty-one, should you decide to indulge,
Be moderate in such things, and sober you should remain.

It is against the law for teenagers to serve or drink,
So to obey the law is always best.
Never drink and drive,
And don't ride with anyone who cannot pass the sobriety test.

Keep from causing accidents that can maim or kill.
It is a heartbreak when young or older lives are taken away,
All because someone drove while intoxicated,
Thinking that driving that way was okay.

When the laws are broken, individuals have to pay for the crime,
And mothers, fathers and friends have reason to cry.
Incarceration makes separation seem hard and long,
And part of the happy Spirit that dwells within seems to die.

DRIVING

When you are old enough to drive a car,
Though you are close at home or afar,
Study the rules of the country, state, or place,
Because laws are different on each highway you face.
It's necessary that you have a license to drive.
And that the auto is insured for all to safely arrive.
Have a licensed driver with you as you first learn.
With needed instruction, a license you may earn.

For safety: good manners and caution use.
Buckle your seat belt, observe the signs and red lights—
Driving privileges do not abuse.

Before you begin, adjust your mirrors for the front and back.
And slow down or stop if the ambulance or police are on your track.
Keep both hands on the wheel to steer,

Keep your eyes on the road; then there's nothing to fear.

Slow down for the curves along the way,
And keep your cell phone off or at bay.

Remember the auto is not a toy.
It is to be driven with care, if you're to enjoy.
Keep within the posted limits for speed.
Avoid getting angry— even if others refuse to heed.
Never drink alcoholic beverages while at the wheel
Or ride with someone who would drink or steal.
The person in the get-away car is usually caught.
So choose legal activities while driving and doing what you ought.

DRIVING (CONTINUED)

Select your passengers with care.
Seldom pick up hitch-hikers, your car to share.
You never know what they will do.
They might have your cash and car before you are through.
Many accidents may end with a crash,
And death or injuries can come quickly— in a flash.
Then be careful and cautious when you drive,
If you want to be safe and get there alive.

Be careful and cautious when you drive
So you don't cause an accident and will arrive alive.

COOPERATION IS THE KEY

Don't be afraid of the officers of the law.
They will not use their gun, unless there's cause for a draw.
Even then, they are trained in their use.
They use their equipment with care, not abuse.

If you are quite ill or are threatened, call 9-I-I.
The ambulance or patrol will come on the run.
Be sure it's an emergency before you call,
And be specific so there will be no cause to stall.

The officers are there to help and protect wherever you are:
On the road, at home or afar.
Let the answers you give be honest and true;
And be polite and cooperative in what you say and do.
So if you are ever stopped by the police,
Be courteous and respectful before your release.

A CAMP FOR YOUTH

A handsome football player
And a physically challenged girl
Were attending a camp for youth
Where goals and thoughtful ways were unfurled.

The campers sat quietly and listened;
They heard how they should treat others;
But actions speak louder than words,
And some forget they are to act as kind sisters and brothers.

As the handsome football player played,
He was having a very good time;
But when he saw what was happening,
He came from the game, just in time.

The physically challenged girl
Was being pushed and being called ugly names.
A crowd was making fun of her!
It was certainly not approved sportsman-like games.

The handsome football player
Pushed through the crowd to make his way,
When he reached the physically challenged girl,
He had a lot he wanted to say.

A CAMP FOR YOUTH (CONTINUED)

He put his arm around the girl.
He hugged her and held her tight.
He looked at the crowd who was calling names
And said, "This is my camping sister,
so let's treat her right."

"You don't have to call her ugly names,
You don't have to push or shove.
She has feelings and has suffered hurt,
And others are judging you for your lack of love."

"You need to ask forgiveness for what you've done,
And be kind to one another.
We must treat all of our friends and neighbors
As valued fellow-beings, sister and brother."

THERE'S BEAUTY IN A GOOD DANCE

There is beauty in a good dance.
There can be grace, talent and charm.
There can be rhythm in each step—
If done with dignity, it can do no harm.

There are many different kinds of dances.
Many include techniques with spins or skips.
Ballroom dancing is smooth and pretty,
But here are some very timely tips.

Avoid dancing in ways that offend.
It's not "cool" or funny to cause a disgrace.
Your parents and friends might be watching
And would not be pleased when they see your face.

Learn new dance steps to gain favor—
As long as they won't defame your good name.
Remember, a good name is better
Than an indecent dance or a quest for ill fame.

ANIMALS AND PETS

If you have pets, be kind to them.
Feed them and give them clean water each day.
They have needs and feelings too
And need to be cared for in a loving and gentle way.

Animals were put here with a purpose in mind.
Some are for pets or for food.
They bring love and usefulness we find.

Cruelty to all animals is against the law.
Be kind to each living creature.
Abuse to animals is a crime
And can be reason to be fined or confined.
Keep the law!

BE NEAT AND ORDERLY

There was a beautiful young lass
Who was the smartest in her class.
She'd meet friends who always came
To see her when she seemed a dream.

But their calls became their last.
Her loveliness always faded fast.
How could an otherwise fair queen
Keep a house like hers—unsightly, unclean!

The first impression proved to be wrong.
Beauty was skin deep; she was just head strong.
For pretty is as pretty does,
And it doesn't take long for friends to "buzz."

They found that she was lazy and full of conceit.
They found that her grooming was all but neat.
They saw that she was selfish and grasping for all.
After they befriended her, they soon let her fall.

There were often days that she wondered why
All of her friends soon said goodbye.
When everyone else had such a good time,
They treated her like she wasn't worth a dime.

Her friends talked about her behind her back.
How nice she could be if she were not so slack!
When the word got around how her room was kept,
The story came back to her and she fretted and wept.

After her cry she decided she'd do better.
She wrote her resolutions in a letter.
She started putting her things away—
Hanging her clothes, making her bed each day.

BE NEAT AND ORDERLY
(CONTINUED)

She'd straighten her desk, get ready for school.
She'd study etiquette and know each rule.
She'd help wash the dishes and assist her mother.
She was kinder and more helpful to her younger brother.

Her home became straight; she could hold her head high.
No longer were friends ashamed or shy,
For when she swept around her own step,
Her whole personality was better kept.

Though things are seldom what they seem,
Self-respect and pride can help realize a dream.
A belief in self and a gentle heart
With kindness to others is a good start.

So if you're a lass and a would-be queen,
Live a life of order: be neat and clean.
Look after your room and clean that shelf.
You'll find that even you will like yourself.

A HUNGRY CHILD SEEKS

There was a little boy in elementary school
Who was poor but seldom broke a rule.
But when it was time for the pupils to eat,
He'd joined a "lunch bunch" to beg for a treat.

This boy was not a "Pollyanna."★
He'd come right out and say, "I want that banana."
Or he would say, "You know my parents are not rich.
Come on and give me that sandwich."

Some of us felt sorry for him.
He was hungry and his pickings were often slim.
He and his family were invited to church and Sunday School,
Where the Ten Commandments were taught and the
Golden Rule.

There the boy learned that we should not
"want" what other people own,
And should not either try to ask for things on loan.
Also we should work for that which we desire,
And do only legal work when available for hire.

After that lesson the very next day,
The little boy had taken note and time to pray.
He spoke these words, (I'll never forget):
"I wish I had a banana, which I don't know how to get."

★Pollyanna – One who finds good in most everything.

A HUNGRY CHILD SEEKS
(CONTINUED)

Some of us then shared our food,
Because we were all in a generous mood.
We had told our parents and they included extra food for him,
And he became a happy child and said, "Thanks!" with a grin.

It was wonderful how his attitude had changed.
He was accepted more by others; he was no longer estranged.
So when you are looking for help from a friend,
Remember to be grateful and polite: on
you blessings will descend.

FOOD AND NUTRITION

Food is an important part of living,
But you need to eat what is good for you.
Junk food is not the best for your health;
Then let's review what is good to eat and do.

We should choose foods that do not irritate,
Foods that are good for body, mind and soul.
Limited amounts for three to five meals a day are recommended.
Some foods should be served hot and others cold.

We have learned that "You are what you eat,"
And to choose your food wisely is a good thing to do.
A variety of greens and red are good choices,
And you'll be more energetic when you choose a few.

Try to eat meals with your family—
Once or twice a day.
Let it be a place of greetings and pleasant conversation.
You'll find this time together will really pay.

Convey what you like about sports;
Describe a show, a course, or activities on the courts.
Tell about an incident at school or at work you enjoyed.
Discuss current events, a hobby, or a job you'd like when employed.

Make good food choices that end up on your plate.
Dairy products and meat are enjoyed in moderation as a start.
Then there is bread, cereal, rice, pastas, carrots,
greens, bananas and grapes.
These grains, vegetables and fruits should
make up your diet's biggest part.

Eat small amounts of butter, margarine, oils and sweets.
But it's good to eat two or three servings a day
Of milk products, meat, poultry, fish, dried beans, eggs and nuts.
This is called eating the food guide— pyramid's way.

WAYS POSSIBLY TO AVOID CANCER

Scientists believe that unbalanced foods that we eat
Are the leading causes of at least two-thirds of cancer from our diet.
Most of the remaining one-third is caused from smoking.
The best protection is eating the right foods, so let's try it.

When we go shopping for groceries,
Look for apples, bananas, broccoli and whole grains;
Many of the plant foods work together
To give us a protective climate inside our bodies and brains.

There are free radicals running rampant in our bodies.
They attack the healthy cells and pave a way.
Not stopped, they will cause a chain reaction
For cancers or tumors to develop with free radical attacks each day.

Now some free radicals can be avoided,
If we do not smoke or breathe cigarette smoke.
Pollution and a long time out in the sun
Will also do their dirty work, as it has for some other folk.

Antioxidants are nature's best way that's been found
To stop the free radicals for you and me.
Let's include in our diet beta-carotene and lycopene
And compounds that include vitamins C and E.

Then let's eat plenty of fruits and vegetables.
Let's eat them before radicals have chance to do harm.
Good health is a must if we're to do our best work and play.
Let's eat fresh fruits, vegetables and grains, grown down on the farm.

Information above was taken from the Health & Wellness Reference
Library, "Food for Health and Healing."

WHAT DO YOU DO WHEN NO ONE IS WATCHING?

What do you do when no one is watching?
Would you take a chance and steal?
Would you lie about it afterwards?
How long do you think this act you could conceal?

What do you do when completing reports?
Are you honest or do you plagiarize the facts?
Or do you rejoice when getting away with deceit?
What will you do later if working on your income tax?
What do you do when you're taking a test?
Do your eyes drift around here and there?
Do you think others should tell you the answers?
Or do you think you should work, study and thus prepare?

If you know that someone is planning to kill,
And you know that the threat is real,
Do you tell a responsible person,
Or do you decide the truth you'll not reveal?

If someone should ask you to use or sell drugs,
Would you say, "No," or "Yes"?
Would you report it to your parents and then police?
Or would you be silent and not profess?

When you are sick and go to a doctor,
Do you want to go to the very best?
Would you want to go to one who had cheated?
Or do you want one who has passed every lab work and test?

People are different from other creatures.
They are given the right to think, make choices and to speak.
Then act responsibly in whatever you say and do.
You have to live with yourself; so earn
respect; be strong in all you seek.

BE A GOOD COMMUNICATOR

When you speak, say what you mean.
Avoid gossip about others; use restraint.
Say only what is good about someone,
And your reputation will be good, without complaint.

Take what others say about you with a grain of salt.
You know the honest truth.
That is really what ever matters;
Keep the right values you've learned from youth.

Some people will say and do things
That might hurt or make you want to cry.
Don't become full of revenge or anger,
Because parents, educators, or the Courts
will take care of things bye and bye.

If you don't understand an issue or subject,
Ask questions and take a stand.
Try to avoid misunderstandings.
Your slow and studied responses will be in demand.

Give to the world the best that you have,
And in turn, good things will be your part:
Food on the table, shelter and clothes to wear.
You'll be happy from the very start,
And best of all— you'll have peace in your heart.

LET YOUR SPEECH BE CLEAN

Be careful of what comes out of your mouth.
Let your speech be clean and worthy to repeat.
Avoid the use of profane or obscene language.
It's not necessary to use words that come from the street.

What you say lets others know from where you've come.
They can usually tell if you are a drop-out from school.
Many will judge you from what you write or say,
So study and practice good English and try to follow each rule.

Try to think before you speak.
Put your mind in gear before your mouth gets into motion.
When you start looking for a good job,
Good speech and language could lead to earning a promotion.

When others excel by doing quite well,
Write them a letter and give them a pat on the back.
Tell them how much you admire them as you offer praise—
Avoid words you'd later wish to retract.

What you say betrays your character.
Your words influence others or they might offend.
Be true to your God and to yourself,
And you'll gain respect of family and friend.

KEEP YOURSELF
ON THE RIGHT TRACK

As you grow older, keep on the right track.
Avoid letting your *mind take a wrong turn.
Evade getting angry, because you are right.
Or success has failed to come for
which you did yearn.

There is something good in most situations,
So look for the best you can find.
There are values you can give to someone else—
A listening ear, a cheering up, or a sharing of mind.

Stress can weigh you down, no doubt.
It can be a serious matter.
If you won't care about the topic a few years from now,
Move on; forget the negative and useless chatter.

Calm down by taking a deep breath.
Close your eyes and imagine the problem has gone away.
Drink something hot like tea, cocoa or water,
And you'll find you will have a happier and more peaceful day.

"The one who ask questions doesn't lose
his way." —African Proverb

Information for the poem above was gleaned from the Internet, Belief.
Five Ways to Stay on Track by Henrik Edberg.

BROADEN YOUR OUTLOOK

The problem with self-absorption
Is a lack of balance between love of others and self.
A person needs to broaden his or her outlook
By seeking fellowship and reading a
good book from off the shelf.

You'll need to choose interests outside your home.
And participate in service learning, a charity,
4-H Club or becoming a Scout.
These efforts will broaden your outlook and be meaningful,
And the leadership experience will mean a lot, no doubt.

Give to a place or charity that will help others,
If you receive any pay.
Remember to set some of your funds aside
For the future's possibly rainy day.

Observe certain customs of politeness.
Always knock before opening a closed door.
Respect the mail and rights of others.
Listen and respond, but don't ever become a bore.

Find a hobby that you really enjoy.
It can be collecting items, working in a garden, or playing sports.
It can be reading, boating or fishing,
By yourself or with joining friends and cohorts.

Life is so full of the possible—
Achieving, helping others, doing your best.
It's up to you to study and work hard,
Because love, faith, hope, and peace should be your quest.

USE YOUR TIME WISELY

Use your time wisely each day.
Do your work first and then you can play.
Perform any kindness that you can.
Develop good work habits for success to command.

The old saying of "Early to bed and early to rise
Makes a person healthy, wealthy and wise,"
Still holds true today.
Another sage has said, "You are what you eat and drink each day."

Remembering others, we are told,
Will cause us to have love and peace in our hearts when we are old.
What do you want said about yourself when you are gone?
That you did what was right—instead of wrong?

Time marches on, so do your best,
And you'll do well when you take that final test.
You can hear your family and friends say, "Well done,"
And a place in heaven you may have won.

SAY IT WITH FLOWERS

A flower garden is filled with mirth
Where bluebirds sing throughout the earth.
Each flower holding its head up high
Can speak of love or days gone by.

Pretty flowers swaying in the breeze,
Choose the right one and you're sure to please.
"Be cautious," says the yellow Golden Rod,
But Ivy gives friendship a good luck nod.

Pretty flowers swaying here, I see.
The Verbena says, "Please pray for me."
Then there's the little blue For-get-me-not
That seems to say, "I haven't forgot."

The language of flowers can express
A dream of love and happiness.
If words don't come, then send a bouquet.
It will brighten a beloved one's special day.

Pretty flowers, large and small—
I'm fondest of the one that's sweetest of them all.
It's the red, red ROSE that rings so true.
It's the flower that says, "I love you."

WORK, SAVE AND BUDGET

We need money in order to acquire
Many things that life requires.
We need shelter, food, and clothes;
Too we need the fulfillment of other desires.
If we read the Book of Proverbs,
We'll find our needs depend on our ways and lifestyle.
We'll find that the amount available to us
Is through our work and gifts that make life worthwhile.

We should not gain wealth through fraud or swindle,
But through honest practices, plans and ways.
Blessings will come to those who work and give freely
And will thus be happy with themselves for all of their days.
Then work and open a bank account.
Put aside and save a little money each week.
Give one-tenth to your church or charity,
And perhaps you'll find the blessings you seek.
Make a budget for our everyday care
And plant many good seeds.
Figure carefully for all of your food, housing and clothing.
Take out insurance for your possible health and accident needs.

Fill your cup with love and hope,
Add a bit of faith and care.
And—remember your loved ones each day
When you go to your God in prayer.

SPORTS

It is good to play all kinds of sports.
They help to develop and train body and mind,
But you must learn and obey the rules of the games—
If you don't want to be left behind.

Ask for a copy of the rules and guides.
Read and study each word and line.
Ask questions should you have any;
Exercise fair play and all will be fine.

Sports can help one to look at life;
Such as, the values of giving and sharing.
Now, if you can't play sports, you can be one
By the way you treat others and by caring.

Play Football, Basketball, Tennis, Baseball, and Soccer.
Each game can be fun whenever you play.
If you work really hard and go professional,
Should you excel, you could earn very good pay.

THE WAY TO TREAT OTHERS

Treat others the way you want to be treated.
Treat them with kindness, in caring and friendly ways.
If you do this, you'll be glad that you did
Without regret in your future days.

You'll not only win friends and influence others,
But you'll find that your conscience within
Will speak to you and let you know
That in what you said and did, you acted as friend to friend.

Treating others the way you want to be treated,
Is often called the "Golden Rule."★
Follow that principle and you'll find
Love, success and respect become your module.

★Golden Rule may refer generally to:

Ethic of reciprocity, the Golden Rule in ethics, morality, history and religion. The Golden Rule was a common principle in ancient Greek philosophy. Examples of the general concept include:

"Do not to your neighbor what you would take ill from him"— Pittacus

"Avoid doing what you would blame others for doing." — Thales

"Do not do to others what would anger you if done to you by others." Isocrates

References referring to the Golden Rule may be found in Leviticus 19:18; Matthew 7:12; and Luke 6:31, among other books of the Holy Bible.

Source is **from Wikipedia, the free encyclopedia.**

FORGIVENESS

Forgiveness is the smile you give although you hurt inside.
Forgiveness is the second mile you walk with love, not pride.
Forgiveness is your steady hand without a backward glance.
Forgiveness is just knowing that there is another chance.

Forgiveness is the sunshine that comes after rain.
Forgiveness is the way a crushed flower blooms again.
Forgiveness is the calm after all the storms have gone.
Forgiveness is taking time to listen to a quiet but lovely song.

Forgiveness is to understand and not condemn a person's ways.
Forgiveness is forgetting and then finding words of praise.
Forgiveness, one may ask of you, then you humbly bow in prayer,
And as you ask forgiveness, you will find forgiveness there.

CHILD MOLESTER LAWS

No matter how old you are
And you touch a person in an inappropriate way,
You could be punished, placed on probation or go to prison;
Or you might never again see the light of day.

It is often better to keep your hands to yourself;
To violate the body of others is crude.
If you think and stop before you act,
Then in Court, you will not be sentenced or sued.

Be aware of older strangers and the gifts they might give
Or a lot of money they might offer to pay.
You don't know what they might do to your body.
It is better to say, "NO!" and then run away.

There are good touches and bad touches.
There are consensual and non-consensual acts.
Refrain from becoming a sexual offender or a sexual predator
By studying and learning the admonition in the legal facts.

Show respect for your body and that of others.
Find out when and if it's acceptable to give a loving touch with
the hand.
You can always congratulate others with a gentle pat on the back.
That's a gesture that most all will understand.

Avoid touching others inappropriately
Or in a way that you, yourself, would not like.
You can forever avoid going to prison—
If you always do what is right.

IT IS BETTER TO WAIT

It is better to wait for sex until you marry,
Because more than one partner can be a cause for fear.
Venereal diseases are transmitted to others
And can be given to those whom you hold dear.
Protected and unprotected sex can often give cause for alarm.
Unwanted and unplanned pregnancies frequently come about.
Serious decisions will then have to be made—
Just check with your medical doctor— in case there is doubt.

Some diseases can be transferred through the lips of a kiss,
Or from those who have unprotected hands.
If you have sex only with your spouse, you could be free from disease
No matter if you are at home or in foreign lands.
Major venereal diseases are caused by germs.
They can be a menace to everyone around.
Every case comes from another case.
Without treatment the infection will
spread—could be even death bound.

Venereal diseases can invade the body.
Blood work is necessary to determine the cause.
There can be inflammation of the eyes, heart, mouth and
of the joints.
This should be enough to make one stop or pause.
Some of the transmitted sexual diseases
Are Syphilis, Gonorrhea, AIDS, and HIV.
Then protect yourself from these diseases:
Study the facts and live a lifestyle that will leave you disease free.

(The information above has been gleaned from various medical and
health journals, encyclopedias and from listening to seminars with
medical professional personnel).

IF WE SHOULD FALL IN LOVE

If we should fall in love with someone and find
That differences are very great,
Then we have to decide what is right for each other.
We need to do what is best before it's too late.

We should not lose our faith and love for humankind,
Even though we are led in separate ways.
We can still have respect for each other—
Even though we do not share our days.

Let us be happy in what we do,
And remember that love never comes by force.
If we should find that love is not mutual,
Then we should seek a new way and plot a new course.

Although some marry for money or companionship,
Others may marry to escape from home.
It is better to avoid divorce and not marry,
If the partner has eyes that constantly roam.

Look for friends or a partner who is unselfish and outgoing.
Find those who are wholesome and have faith and hope in you.
Then on the bottom line you will find that those you love,
Will wish you happiness and success in all that you do.

WHEN YOU WISH TO GET MARRIED

"To have friends, one must be friendly"
Is an often quoted phrase.
If you are kind, honest and have high ideals,
Friends will seek you out and offer praise.

Being sincere of purpose and being unselfish
Are other traits that endure.
Patience and an interest in others
Are characteristics and features of which you can be sure.

Set high and noble goals for your life.
As you mature, study the lives of those you most admire.
When you are capable of making your own decisions,
You'll seek friends who are loyal and inspire.

Then when the time comes that you wish to get married,
After a good education and finding a job,
Your kind and good friends will encourage and support you,
Then you'll avoid seeking membership in the mob.

A strong bond in marriage is faithfulness.
Find someone who inspires and motivates you for good.
Marry because you love and want to be together forever,
And don't be tempted by pre-marital sex as some would.

FRIENDSHIP

I want you to know and understand
That my purpose in life is to teach
And to help others to come to know
That true friendship is within their reach.

True friends may be precious and rare,
So let us give them each day our best.
Let us be a friend to others,
For there is no better way to invest.

Let us cherish kind regard for each other
No matter what our wealth or fame;
And in spite of our shortcomings,
May we be friends just the same.

We can be better friends to each other
If we forget and forgive.
We can believe in each other with trust.
We can help each other to love and give.

We can all be good neighbors
If we live by the Golden Rule, ★
And we can all be a little more friendly
At work, at play, at home or at school.

We can extend our appreciation
To those who've given a helping hand.
We can be grateful that we have such good friends
Who are willing to help and to take a stand.

Then as we offer the hand of friendship
And greet each other with a smile,
At the end of the day we'll surely know
That today has been worthwhile.

★Golden Rule – "The rule or principle of treating others as one wants to be treated."

LOVE FOR OUR COUNTRY

At one time, Americans believed in their country.
Although things were not going very well,
They rallied behind and supported their leaders:
They were all in it together, because war is Hell.

The troops were entertained,
The troops' morale to raise.
Their sacrifice we recognized
And their heroism commanded our praise.

Scrap metal was collected,
Rationed were soap, butter and gasoline.
Many bought war bonds.
Citizens gave their time, even many a teen.

If our vote did not elect the President,
He was still followed, right or wrong.
But patriotism and values have changed;
They are not voiced in battle cry and song.

There were no demonstrations against the war.
There were no complaints about the capture and treatment of spies.
The news media supported our armed forces.
There were no divisive theories fraught with lies.

It's still important that we stick and work together
In the good old American way,
Where in schools we started with a Pledge of Allegiance,
And for our troops we'd openly pray.

Let's keep the courage and fortitude of our forefathers
Who loved our country with pride
Let's thank those who are willing to defend and sacrifice,
And remember those who for the cause have died.

LOVE FOR OUR COUNTRY
(CONTINUED)

Times have changed, but freedom still is not free,
And many continue making sacrifices for you and me.
Some have given their lives and others have
been given a Purple Heart.
Yes, many have served, worked and died for our liberty.

Let's show our love for our country
By being good citizens who support and work all day long.
When of age, let's register and vote our convictions
In a way that will help keep Americans unified and strong.

Let's study and review the backgrounds of all candidates.
Read and ask questions before we vote.
Make sure that the changes that are promised
Are good for our country and the best evoke.

Let's be happy that we've had a part
And can show love for our country in a patriotic song.
Let's be thankful that we can vote our convictions,
And all can still pull together to keep America's freedoms strong.

Listen, read and ask questions before you vote.

THE ROAD TO SUCCESS

If we think of a mountain as the road to success,
We'll keep trudging along up hill.
We'll take time to sigh and a time to rest;
Find peace in our hearts and share goodwill.

We may twist and turn as we continue on.
Cares may press down a bit.
Things may go wrong sometimes,
But to succeed, we rest but never quit.

Success is leading and following.
Success is failure turned upside down.
Success is appreciating those who help.
Success is working with no thought of a crown.

Millions may stay at the base of the mountain.
Fear and doubt may make them stop.
But success comes to those who continue to climb,
And along the way, all who help reach the top.

The poem above was first published in Secrets and Songs of Payne's Prairie, Copyright 1998, by Margaret A. Rosenberger, page 48.

BLACK ON BLACK CRIMES

We have Black on Black crime.
There are also Black on Brown crime,
But we should all learn that if we commit a crime,
We have to either pay for or spend in jail some time.

When we are put away in detention or jail,
We can't sleep in our own bed.
We can't see our family members
And tomorrow? We won't know what's ahead.

There's no need for Black on Black crime.
Blacks should all be glad *when* their people of Color succeed.
We might all succeed if we study, work hard and try.
And a handout? Food stamps or Welfare we might not need.

We can have more love and esteem for ourselves with self-respect
When we work for and earn what we desire.
We'll not always look for Government or other assistance,
Though we might never "set the world on fire."

Then let us take each day as it comes.
Be happy when other people work, study and succeed.
If we're responsible, accountable and will apply ourselves,
We'll find that we can earn most of what we want
And all of what we really need.

FOLLOW YOUR DREAM

Keep your body healthy and strong.
If you eat your fruits and veggies,
You won't go wrong.

When night comes, stay off of the street;
Violence and drugs are out there,
So go to bed and get your sleep.

Study the rules of the games of all sports.
Get exercise for yourself:
In the gym, on the playground or on the courts.

Be able to laugh at yourself when you make a mistake.
No one is perfect,
So pick yourself up and another turn take.

Be aware of and stay off of that illegal drug.
It can cause your death or land you in jail.
Then avoid becoming an addict or being a thug.

The use of tobacco can be way out of line.
It can cause diseases and other cares,
So if you use tobacco, stop it in time.

To have fun, alcoholic beverages you don't have to drink.
Besides you can lose self-control,
Become an addict, or not be able to think.

Remember to rest and find time to meditate.
If you are headed for surgery or a hospital stay,
Spiritual help could calm your fears along the way.

FOLLOW YOUR DREAM
(CONTINUED)

A large network of family and friends who support
Can help you feel less anxiety and pain.
Seek their support and know that you're
not alone and that you can regain.

Avoid the temptation to cheat or steal.
Work for what you get,
Then your self-respect can be real.

Always try to be honest and true,
And show love for others
In how you act and what you say and do.

When you really love others, you will do no harm.
You will always find
That hate and anger have no charm.

If you make a promise, do your best to keep your word.
Refuse to fail and disappoint others.
Being credible is much preferred.

When it is time to choose a career,
Find something you like to do.
Work can then come by doing what is dear.

You can be different and not follow the crowd.
You can be creative and think for yourself.
Kind and sweet thoughts are always allowed.

FOLLOW YOUR DREAM
(CONTINUED)

No matter what others do or how they may seem,
Have a goal and purpose for your own life,
And always follow your dream.

If you'd like to make a note
Or draw a picture here,
Think about what you have read,
And illustrate that dream
Which you hold dear.

OUR INDEPENDENCE

We celebrate our country's independence.
It's a history of freedom and justice, we recall.
We raise our flag: the red, white and blue,
To salute our nation's greatness and uniqueness above all.

We take pride in the Statue of Liberty,
For the huddled masses, it continues a beacon true.
We revere our temples, mosques, churches
And for the brave and lost heroes— their monuments too.

We thank the armed men and women in service today
Who help protect and keep us and our country from harm.
We pray that peace will come into our hearts
And that God will guide our leaders, when there's an alarm.

Then let us do all that we can
To work, give, and volunteer.
As long as we live, there is service to give
To God, mankind, and to our country that we hold so dear.

WE CELEBRATE THE
BIRTHDAY OF AMERICA

We celebrate the birthday of America.
Our Independence Day was proclaimed July 4, 1776.
We have a long and eventful history
In which cultures, backgrounds and races all mix.

We have beautiful patriotic songs
That thrill the hearts and souls of you and me.
The words and the tempo stir the emotions
But, as Americans, our freedom is really not free.

We appreciate all the ones who have fought for our country.
We grieve for those who have been injured or died.
Our thoughts and desires are still with those
Who continue to fight on a foreign country side.

A LESSON IN CIVICS

The defining concept of American History
Was conceived in 1776 when our Founding Fathers broke
With Britain and established a country that would rule itself.
Then let us equip ourselves with wisdom, knowledge
and love as its principles we invoke.

There are three branches of government.
We should all know them, we will agree:
The legislative, executive and judiciary.
They help oil the wheels of democracy.

The First Amendment forbids the establishment
of an official religion.
Our citizens can worship the way they choose.
But our creeds proclaim: "One nation under God."
And with "In God we trust," we cannot lose.

"Life, liberty and the pursuit of happiness" is often proclaimed.
The Declaration of Independence heralds this truth.
We should study these documents in the schools.
And learn to be better citizens from the days of youth.

The words, "Government of the people,
by the people, for the people"
Come from Lincoln's Gettysburg address.
These words should be a source of hope and inspiration
And one with appreciation, for America's the best.

YOU ARE NOT A BRAT

When I taught in Germany in the U. S. Army Dependents' Schools,
I had to study and learn new standards, policies and rules.
But when pupils introduced themselves with "I'm an Army Brat,"
As their teacher, I told them that I did not view them as that.
I asked that we look up that word
To see if that's what they wanted to be.
When they found out what "brat" really meant,
With me, they did agree.

"Brat" in the dictionary—Webster's book—
Meant "a nasty child," when we took a look.
Now, no one wants to be thought of or to be like that,
"Then let's not think of oneself as an Army brat."

I told my class that I saw them as precious—with a great potential
Each and everyone.
I looked forward to working with them
In study, music and fun.
We need to find as we get a little older
That we are responsible for ourselves,
And with self-esteem, we might get a little bolder.
We need to have respect for ourselves and others,
If we really want to succeed.
Kind words turn away anger,
Good deeds and works can help meet many a need.
Think of yourself made from the pattern of your mother and father,
And such a treasure in your parents' sight.
They would never see you as a brat,
But ones they love who want to work and do what's right.

ARE SOME STILL ENSLAVED?

During the 1800s, there were slavery days,
And those enslaved were denied a free man's ways.
But their masters gave them their food, housing and clothes.
Most were taught how to work, read and
sing— most everyone knows.

The slaves were freed but another side we should not forget.
The owners' losses were great; requests for help were never met.
Many owners did not get back on their feet;
They went to their graves in poverty and defeat.
Many lives were ruined, but others kept on—
Made their families work, still praised God in song.

Now our government gives food and subsidized rent.
"Free lunches" are provided; some don't pay a cent.
While it's good the poor to help and feed,
But should they expect others to meet each need?
It is good to give the hungry food,
But why don't we teach them to cook food to be baked or stewed?
It is good to give those in need a room,
But can't we teach them to raise veggies or flowers that bloom?

There is a saying I dare to repeat.
"If a man will not work, he shall not eat."
Then let's teach each one how to earn
A self-supporting life—the lessons which they need to learn.
If people keep getting handouts, are they still not enslaved?
Will they ever want to work and earn that for which they crave?

Before pupils graduate from school, let's teach each one a trade,
For work is said to be good for those who make the grade.
Vocational training-education is a good place to start,
But first of all, we need to have a change of heart.

SPEAK THE LANGUAGE

If you're from another country,
And English, you've never learned,
Practice the language with people wherever you are.
The natives will admire you, their respect you will have earned.

The language of most countries contains "parts of speech."
One usage for verbs, is present, past and future tense.
Once you understand their use and purpose,
You'll be less likely to be confused and have more confidence.

If you are a local resident and want to upgrade your status,
To give yourself more class,
Try studying the English language,
And greater opportunities might come to pass.

For example, if you should say, "He done,"
Instead of saying, "He did,"
Or saying, "I seen," instead of "I saw."
These are incorrect, and of these errors do be rid.

He "don't" is another contraction that's a mistake.
It is much better to say, "He doesn't" or "He does not."
Once again, learn the correct way of speaking,
And incorrect contractions from your speech, please blot.

A word that is often said is "hisself."
If you look it up, you'll find there's no such word.
So dust off that Webster on the shelf
Know that for good usage, the word is "himself,"
And don't be a nerd!

SPEAK THE LANGUAGE
(CONTINUED)

Another word that's often used is "ain't."
Instead of saying, "I am" or "I am not."
That is a word that should be buried
In every school yard plot.

At one school, "ain't" was written on pieces of paper
and placed in a jar.
Never was it to be used again.
Those students present will never forget.
"Ain't" was dropped from their vocabulary; it did not remain.

So study, practice, and read good books,
And good manners and grooming heed.
Because of your skills and well-groomed looks,
Others will see that you are polished and will help you succeed.

DARKNESS

Before darkness falls,
It's time to head for home,
Where you can have good food to eat—
There's no reason for you to roam.

There is mischief in the darkness
That you cannot see.
Criminals share the streets
And you don't need their company.

Temptations come in the darkness.
Unlawful bribes and offers are often made.
Many times people are killed—
Or they are threatened and made afraid.

Drugs are sold in the darkness—
And sometimes in the daylight.
You don't need that kind of traffic;
So try to do what's right.

If there is a game to play at school at night,
Or if there is a school activity to share,
Go, and then head for home.
Darkness holds dangers of which you are unaware.

Now you need not be afraid of the darkness,
When you are in your parents' house.
You find comfort in the familiar,
And it offers safety— your own good guardhouse.

When darkness comes,
You should sleep in your own bed.
So don't hang out on the streets,
Because to danger you may be led.

KEEP ON KEEPING ON

Be like the duck— keep paddling along
And keep in your heart a beautiful song.
Keep positive thoughts in your intelligent mind.
Seek company with those who are good and kind.

Study hard and practice doing what's right.
Ignore those who may offend or slight.
Look for work that pleases you.
Be loyal and honest, dependable and true.

Give to the world the best you have,
And you'll find there is merit in this healing salve.
Be a good steward in what you make,
For it's the love of money, we should forsake.

Let's support leaders who are morally strong;
With good examples, we can follow along.
Then let's turn off the tube on the TV set
Or when offensive words, acts, or violence are on the Internet.

Let's love our country but hate war.
If we have to fight, let's know what it's for.
But if we can't have peace in the world about,
We can have it within— there is no doubt.

Then let us "keep on keeping on."
And keep in our hearts' a lovely song.
If we practice these things, we should have a good life.
One that is happy and free of strife.

This poem has been revised, but it is dedicated to the memory of my
brother Ralph Franklin Rosenberger who died in Valdosta, Georgia, on
April 21, 1985. He would have been 60 on May 23rd of that year. One of the
last things he said to me was: "I hope that you will keep on keeping on."

PRACTICE GOOD HYGIENE

Much can be said about good hand washing.
Much more than you might think.
There are steps to follow for good hand-washing hygiene,
Also for exercise, healthy eating and for milk and juices you drink.

When you wash your hands,
Remember your fingers, thumbs and each nail.
Lather with soap; then rinse with warm running water.
Make this a habit — without fail.

Dry your hands completely with a clean towel.
Use a clean paper towel to turn the water off.
Refrain from washing in a basin of standing water—
Good hygiene practices, do not scoff.

Now when you cough or sneeze,
It is better to cover your mouth with your arm—
Rather than with your hand.
You'll then pass on fewer germs and do less harm.

We need to keep from influenza and other infections
By always practicing good hygiene.
Then let's ALL wash our hands frequently:
Remember to keep our hands and bodies nice and clean,

Source: Centers for Disease Control and Prevention and *The Gainesville Sun,* May 1, 2009.

THERE IS MUCH TO LEARN AND DO

When I taught school,
The pupils would not eat butter.
They did not know how it was made,
And the things they said about butter made me shudder.

So I bought some cream and poured it in a jar.
The pupils took turns at shaking and churning it.
They ate the butter on hot biscuits at lunch,
And it was enjoyed— every morsel and bit.

My pupils thought that they knew
That milk came only from a large store.
They didn't know that milk came from a cow.
What my pupils didn't know prompted me to teach them more.

A field trip was made to a farm—
To let them see horses, sheep and cows.
They watched the farmer milk a cow
And all I heard was loud "WOW'S."

My pupils thought that peanuts fell from trees like pecans.
I just had to put my pupils at ease.
They knew a lot about many things,
But peanuts do not grow on trees.

We went to a farm where peanuts were grown,
And my pupils pulled the plants up from the ground.
They picked peanuts from off the roots.
My pupils were amazed as they worked or looked all around.

Now, if you ever want to volunteer or have a part or full-time job,
Or are bored and think you have nothing to do,
Go to a farm where you can work with animals or plants.
You will find the great outdoors might be appealing to you.

WHAT IS ETIQUETTE?

Good etiquette is considering others
Every where you go.
Then try reading and studying etiquette books
And talking to people who are in the know.

There are social and professional ways to act—
Though it be at church, temple, mosque, work or school.
Don't be afraid to ask questions:
Study and be grounded in each and every rule.

Etiquette prescribes correct behavior
In polite society— with love and grace.
Then keep from drawing attention to yourself,
But keep a smile upon your face.

You may go to a high-priced restaurant
Or eat at a cafeteria not so fine;
But "Keep your elbows off the table,"
A good rule in which manners are defined.

If in doubt, watch the host or hostess as to what is done—
Even to placing a napkin in your lap.
It is better not to complain about the food
Unless in private or to the waiter who is on-tap.

In America, the gentleman helps the lady be seated.
Whether at a table or in a car.
Gentlemen let the ladies go first
Whether at home, at school or afar.

WHAT IS ETIQUETTE?? (CONTINUED)

In conversation, speak clearly and be well-versed in what you
have to share;
But being quiet should never be a chore.
Listening to others is excellent advice
And better than talking too much and becoming a bore.

Be gracious in word, speech and deed.
Remember to say, "Thank you" and "Please,"
"Excuse me" and "I am sorry."
And please cover your mouth when you cough or sneeze.

Be kind and gentle with older people.
They have worked hard and deserve respect.
Bestow decency in speech and conduct—
Tolerance, patience, and care do not neglect.

There are other rules of conduct
Like opening the door for another:
Allowing him or her to go first
Should be routine and be no bother.

Since other people often watch us,
Try to act and practice what's in good taste.
Apply good manners learned in life and education:
Such training will never be a waste.

So if you want to have success in life,
Be gracious and attentive in doing every good deed.
These practices will help your self-confidence.
And, as a person of quality, you can succeed.

VITAMINS A, C AND E

Scientist and nutritional researchers believe
That Vitamins A, C and E
Might be good for preventing cancer, diseases of the heart and
aging.
They've been called "The Big Three."

Vitamin A might can scrub your body of harmful pollutants:
Repair the body's cells and provide a healthy skin
Eating fruits and veggies which are yellow and orange
Are good ways to begin.

Some of these foods include:
Apricots, bok choy, cantaloupe, carrots and kale;
Peaches, spinach, potatoes, pumpkins, mixed veggies and squash.
Eat or take "The Big Three" and never say fail.

If you want to increase your general health,
Increase your intake of Vitamin C.
Supplements are good, but it's better
To go to foods which are rich in Vitamin C; such as, broccoli.

Other foods are strawberries, oranges, mustard greens
and cauliflower,
Cooked cabbage, cantaloups, and brussel sprouts.
Others are pineapple juice, spinach, turnip greens and tomato juice.
Collard greens, grapefruit, and mango, in case there are doubts.
Eat all you can of these foods,
And resistance to deadly diseases will be increased, not reduced.

VITAMINS A, C AND E (CONTINUED)

Vitamin E is also an antioxidant.
It can help with circulation and prevent a blood clot.
Vitamin E is better taken from supplements,
But it's better not to take a lot.

Rather than junk foods, eat fruits and veggies that are rich in
Vitamin A and C. By being healthy, you can become more
handsome or beautiful and strong;
Also you could live longer and have a more productive life.
All of us wish to be happy, successful, and to belong.

Information above was gleaned from *The Book of Powerful Secrets,* **American Publishing Corporation, Copyright 2003, Powerful Secrets.**

CYBER SPACE BULLIES

There are bullies on the Internet,
So be careful when you are on Facebook or other Cyberspace.
Refuse to submit a picture or give personal
information about yourself,
Your family, gender, age or race.

There are several components that lead to a crime:
The opportunity, the ability and a desire.
Don't give anyone the opportunity to hurt you in
your youth or in your prime.
One never knows when on the Internet or
Cyberspace in which others wish to conspire.

There are those who would rob, kill you, or kill
themselves, though not even grown.
Because of a moment of possible excitement and desired joy.
If on Cyberspace, you get a response, requests,
or threats from an unknown,
Tell your parents and inform the police so they might check and
destroy their harmful ploy.
Afterwards, chalk it up to experience,
And, hopefully, from this lesson you will have grown.

FRIENDSHIPS

It's important to have good friends—
Ones who are good for you.
Make sure that they are the right kind
Who will always stand by you.

When you choose your friends,
Make certain that they don't steal;
And when you drive a car,
Make sure you're not intoxicated behind the wheel.

Find friends and be a friend
Who will not end up in jail.
Don't have a friend or be a friend
Who'll have to ask a friend to go his or her bail.

Choose friends who are not into or on drugs
That can destroy your body, mind and soul.
Go into sports, religion, or music,
Where friends and team-spirit can help to make you whole.

Use your wisdom and knowledge
To distinguish between what's right and wrong.
So when you choose your friends,
Choose ones who will help to make you strong.

Good friends are very precious,
But we are told that they are also very rare.
So be sure that the kind of friends you choose:
Good thoughts and ideas you'll always share.

FRIENDSHIPS (CONTINUED)

When choosing friends, you must know
That you are known by the company you keep.
Then choose friends who are thoughtful in things they
say and do—
Ones who will not make you lose your sleep.

Your parents, your siblings and your family
Should be friends with whom you can talk.
Hopefully, they love and care for you
And help you walk the good walk.

Seek friends who have dreams similar to yours:
Ones whose visions and goals are high.
There are those who can give a helping hand
Through honest ways and means, so give them a try.

Find friends that you enjoy being with—
Ones who will help bring you happiness and joy;
Ones who'll bring a smile upon your face,
Because they want to build rather than destroy.

To have friends, one must be friendly;
So try to find one and then be a good friend—
One whom others will want to follow.
Set a good example, and respect and admiration you will surely win.

Always be a considerate friend
Who is honest, kind and true;
And try to find good friends
Who are trustworthy, loyal, and dependable— just like you.

DON'T EVER BE A BULLY

There are many policies and rules
To make sure you and others are safe, free and secure.
Then study, learn and obey them
So that peace and fulfillment for all will endure.

Don't you ever be a bully!
Let me tell you why.
You'll look like a monster
Who doesn't care if others hurt, cry or die.

Bullying and harassment can inflict hurt
And cause others to have psychological distress.
Stalking, written or oral expressions
Can even bring about punishment or arrest.

There's no place for using dehumanizing gestures.
Avoid causing anyone discomfort or performing a humiliating act.
Refrain from making teasing or insulting remarks.
Excluding anyone socially is no way to interact.

Refrain from doing damage or destruction of property.
And, yes, cyberstalking and cyberbullying are wrong—
As are making threats or using intimidating speech.
To a good citizen, they do not belong.

Avoid all violence that is physical.
Defrauding and theft are also criminal acts—
As are harassments that are sexual, religious or racial.
Avoid possible trouble by learning the legal and moral facts.

Remember that no one is quite like you.
Each one is miraculously unique.
No one has the same fingerprints, mind or body,
So appreciate the differences in every relationship you might seek.

DON'T EVER BE A BULLY
(CONTINUED)

Kind words and acts will never die—
Few though they be.
Tell a person if you like what she/he has done.
You'll be glad you did, you'll see.

Now if you should become a victim of or the subject of a bully,
Report him or her to your parents, guardian, teacher,
principal and/or adult friend.
There are consequences for all such offenses,
So be vigilant and be aware of those who
are guilty and willfully offend.

Investigations of reported criminal acts will be made.
Law enforcement agencies should be called in.
Each one will be given due process,
Whether a student, teacher, pastor, friend or kin.

The rights of students, parents and school employees
Are protected by the First Amendment to the Constitution.
Since each life has a meaning and purpose,
Set high goals for yourself, and let this be your resolution:

"Don't ever be a bully; always stay in control
Of your body, mind and soul.
Remember: half of success is a good try;
Then use your talents and aim high.
You can be happy and successful— bye and bye."

Appreciation is expressed to Dr. Charles Hall, Director, Title I, Alachua County Schools, for providing the School Board of Alachua County's Bylaws and Policies (5517.01- Bullying and Harassment) and the Florida Department of Education Model Policy (June 2008); Adopted 7/17/07 and Revised 12/16/08. The above informational poem is based on the contents of those Bylaws and Policies.

LET'S LIMIT OUR TIME ON COMPUTERS

Most of us have a computer
And other forms of electronics;
But it's important to know when and how to use them—
If their uses are to be more harmonic.

Some psychologists and medical doctors
Predict that the computers we use
Might cause us to have serious problems,
If us and our computers we happen to abuse.

We can Twitter, Text, or go on the Internet;
We can use E-mail in any context.
But steady use of a computer
Could cause a person to become an addict.

If we sit at a computer all day,
We might neglect other responsibilities or work.
Our head and back can start aching;
While other duties it's easy to shirk.

Then let us limit our time on the computer
And expand our interests by getting more exercise, study and rest.
We can have a more healthy body and a happier heart
And prove to ourselves and others that we are at our best.

TEASING

Most everyone has been teased
In one way or another.
It can either make you angry or you can laugh about it:
Accept it like an annoyance of a brother.

Often teasing is used, because you're loved—
Or because others admire or are jealous of you.
But you know what you're like deep inside,
So don't be upset at what others say and do.

We are told not to judge others,
So if you're teased, try to turn it all around.
Agree with the teasers and laugh:
Give them a smile instead of a frown.

If teasing can point out a weakness
That you can change or begin anew;
Then accept teasing as a challenge
And positive changes can thus ensue.

A serious kind of teasing can come if you
give out personal information
While chatting or posting pictures on the Internet.
Friendly criminals might be looking or browsing for you.
Never meet strangers posing as friends— or you will regret.

If you are teased and it really bothers you,
Tell your teacher, parent or an adult friend.
Sharing the hurt can help your feelings.
They may act to bring the teasing to an end.

Adults can explain to the teasers
That what they are doing is wrong.
They should direct their energy and words
Into working, studying or singing a song.

TEASING (CONTINUED)

Most teasing can be ignored,
So pay no attention and keep going at a determined pace.
There's no reason to punish or use a knife or gun,
When it would only hurt you and make you lose in life's race.

If you don't like to be teased,
Then you should leave teasing alone.
Treat others the way you want to be treated,
And find the best inner peace you've ever known

Teasing is often displayed in different ways—
How you talk, how you look, or fun about your race.
How it's hard to change the way you are made,
So keep on keeping on, with a pleasant smile upon your face.

THE POLICE

There are different lines of work
That the police are called to do;
Such as, serving on a SWAT★ team, in narcotics, with K9
Or with the CSI Unit,★★ as an investigator too.
The police have had to attend classes;
They have had to study, exercise and train.
When they are assigned to public schools,
They counsel, protect, and teach where safety should reign.

When we see a policeman or woman in uniform, so neat and clean,
Running or speeding down the street,
That action is more than meets the eye.
The officers daily risk their lives, our safety to keep.
If we happen to be driving and hear a siren
Or see blue flashing lights coming from behind,
Let us be obedient, polite and courteous as we pull over
And listen to the officer as we're told what's on his or her mind.

The police have friends and family members
And feelings very much like mine and yours:
They should be treated with respect and courtesy,
Our appreciation should be one that endures
The police are known to many as "Officer Friendly."
Such an officer is surely our guardian and friend.
Our esteem and gratitude for him or her
Should never, ever end.

★SWAT - Special Weapons and Tactics - ★★CSI - Crime Scene
Investigation

NEVER MAKE FALSE ACCUSATIONS

As you grow older, but still in the days of your youth,
Always be true to yourself and tell the truth.
Never make false accusations against parents or friends—
Or even someone you love— if that relationship ends.

A good name is to be chosen more than silver and gold;
So say "NO" to shady deals or knowingly repeat
lies that you've been told.
In case your parents or others are leading you astray,
Be sure you know the "why's" and "where
fore's" before you have your say.

Never make-up things that didn't happen in order to get even
or to make a show of might.
Remember that "Two wrongs will never make a right."
Making false accusations could get you into
trouble—even land you in jail,
And there might not be anyone who would go your bail.

STEALING IS WRONG

All of us live by certain values, standards and principles.
One is a decision to steal or not to steal.
It is much better to buy or earn what you want
Than have to live with yourself and miss-steps conceal.

There are policies, laws and Commandments to obey.
To embezzle, defraud or to heist are wrong.
Other criminal acts are larceny, burglary and theft.
Do not add these bad acts to your life; they do not belong.

Another way of stealing is to cheat.
When you copy from someone else on a test,
You are not passing on your own.
You're not learning and not doing your best.

A different way of stealing is to plagiarize.
You say that this work is your very own,
When actually you're not telling the truth:
It's copied and another name has been shown.

Other ways of stealing are to kidnap—
Or be a robber or a pirate at sea;
Or to poach, seize, and snatch.
They're all misdeeds on which we can agree.

You don't want to end up as someone
Who has landed himself or herself in jail.
It's better to be honest and true to yourself,
Then to your family and friends, you will not fail.

There are more ways that one can steal,
But it's better to make your own way.
Face the world with a guilt-free mind.
Too, respect others who have worked hard to earn their pay.

IF YOU ARE ADDICTED

If you are doing drugs and are addicted,
Let me tell you what to do.
First, confess to your parents and your doctor;
Then tell the police who is selling the drugs to you.

You haven't the remotest idea
What your addiction can cause.
You must know that your parents and family members are hurting,
Because you're ruining your life and violating the laws.

You may be young, beautiful or handsome
And in high school or in college,
But prescription or street drugs can make you opt out
Of your good mind and deny use of your hard earned knowledge.

You can hurt by falling away
From your home and normal life.
You can have illicit sexual encounters
That will lead to pressure, illness, or a life of strife.

You can either end up being alive,
Going to a recovery area or jail.
Other options are being dead and in the cemetery,
And that will be the end of a short-lived tale.

Then look at what you've done
To your loving father, mother, grandfather and grandmothers—
Also to your church, school and community
When you do drugs, you hurt yourself, as well as others.

Please leave that drug environment!
Do whatever it takes to escape the drugs' snare.
Your family and friends want to welcome you home;
They'll extend you every loving care.

The above poem was written after watching the Dr. Phil show on CBS
T-V, April 21, 2009.

SENIOR CITIZENS

If people live long enough
To reach the Golden Age,
They might not be as sharp as they once were,
But there's still a place for them in their pilgrimage.

Most senior citizens are generally retired
From what they used to do,
But that doesn't mean their minds are worn out,
Though their bodies are far from being like new.

They still have dreams and visions
Of how the world should be.
They still have the desire to vote—
An expression of gratitude for their liberty.

Some senior citizens still like to play golf,
Bridge and Bingo, or work at the computer or Jig-saws;
Others like to go for a ride in the country side
Or watch TV or Westerns featuring outlaws.

Many senior citizens like to go to church or synagogue—
The place of worship they choose.
Others like to visit friends or relatives
Where they can relax and discuss the news.

There are those who like to sew,
Play or sing songs that have a pretty tune.
Some senior citizens like letters or stories to write;
While others like to wait for the mail that's "coming soon."

SENIOR CITIZENS (CONTINUED)

Some senior citizens enjoy working with crafts or wood
Or using water colors or oils as a work of art.
Others like to collect, entertain or help
Youth and others make a fresh start.

Some seniors citizens get lonesome
And long for company.
So when you have some time to spare,
Visit them while you're free.

Many seniors have arthritis or trouble in their backs, hips or knees.
Though they may not be able to walk the walk,
You can rest assured
They can still talk the talk.

Now you can see that senior citizens
May have aches and pains,
But they have a positive outlook
And seldom do they complain

Then treat senior citizens the way you'd want to be treated
When you become old and gray.
And you'll have a warm feeling inside
When their wishes you try to obey.

Treat senior citizens with respect.
Try to understand their changing ways.
Be gentle, patient and kind,
And "doing unto others" might reward your Golden Days.

FRUSTRATIONS OF YOUTH

Some teenagers can become frustrated and seek attention.
They look for ways to gain affection.
They feel that they have no one who understands;
They have no one to give them direction.

Often teens are looking for love—
If they lack a good mother/father model or role;
Or they might even feel rebellious—
Not inspired to set life's goal.

There are many reasons why
Teens feel that they have to go their own way,
Though at times, they can get caught up in a gang,
Where drugs or alcohol are freely in play.

When parents fail to take their children
To worship a Higher Being,
They can become self-centered,
Not understanding the teaching they're receiving.

Consequently, teens become sexually active,
The results of which they have no clue.
Because when they become pregnant,
Their joyous days of youth are over— through!

Women are usually responsible for their own bodies,
And it is better for them to observe abstinence and self-control.
If one waits to have sex until he or she marries,
There can be a trusting couple with a happy heart and soul.

FRUSTRATIONS OF YOUTH
(CONTINUED)

Always remember what you were once taught:
The morals, standards and values once learned.
Hopefully, these lead to making the right decisions—
Adhering to principles of right—
unwholesome choices spurned.

Should you fall, you're pregnant, and you refuse to abort,
And you still don't know what to do,
Many couples are waiting with open arms to adopt
Which could be a great blessing for you two.

Call the toll free numbers.
And at Safe-Haven for Newborns, you can drop the infant off,
Though the baby should be seven days old or younger.
Since there is complete anonymity, others cannot scoff.

A SAFE HAVEN FOR NEWBORNS: 1-877-767-BABY (2229)

BE CAREFUL OF WHAT YOU SAY

The poem below is one I found among my mother's papers and creative writings. It explains in verse her philosophy about gossip and criticizing others.

In speaking of a person's faults,
Pray don't forget your own;
Remember those with homes of glass
Should seldom throw a stone.

If we have nothing else to do
But talk of those who sin,
`Tis better that we commence at home
And from that point begin.

We have no right to judge a man
Until he's fairly tried;
Should we not like his company,
We know the world is wide.

Some may have faults . . . and who has not,
The old as well as young . . .
Perhaps we may, for aught we know,
Have fifty to their one.

I'll tell you of a better plan.
You'll find it works quite well.
To try our own defect to cure
Before of others' we tell.

And though I sometimes hope to be
No worse than some I know,
My own shortcomings bid me let
The faults of others go.

BE CAREFUL OF WHAT YOU SAY
(CONTINUED)

Then let us all when we commence
To slander friend or foe,
Think of the harm one word would do
To those we little know.

Remember curses, sometimes,
Like our chickens, "roost at home."
Don't speak of their faults until
We have none of our own.

Lillian A. Rosenberger

LIMIT YOUR TIME ON TELEVISION

If you are really interested in learning
And having a life that is successful and good,
Leave the television in your home off,
And study and read good books, as you should.

Research has been made regarding children's
and youth's watching TV.
Less well will they do in their studies.
Less well do they enjoy family and friends:
They become anti-social and have fewer good buddies.

There are those who have found that watching TV
Is not good for you health-wise.
You could become obese or develop Attention Deficient Disorders
Or other problems in your future that may arise.

There is much violence in movies and in advertising
That is viewed on the TV screen.
It's probably not helpful for anyone to see,
Even though you're older than sweet sixteen.

Although the TV has its place,
It's no substitute for study after school.
Get snacks, exercise, prepare your lessons, and go to bed early.
Making a schedule for yourself is a good rule.

Then limit your time for television viewing.
Listen to the radio and books and newspapers read.
Eat healthy and exercise each day,
And with a purpose for your life, you can succeed.

Part of the information and ideas above are based on "Speaking Out,
Turn off your TV," in *The Gainesville Sun* on April 21, 2009. The article
was written by Arun Egon, principal of the Healthy Learning Academy,
Gainesville, Florida.

DISABILITIES

People—and this includes children—with disabilities
Still have hopes and dreams.
They should be treated normally as any other person,
No matter how great the difficulty seems.
If a person is in a wheelchair,
It doesn't mean that she or he is sick.
Many children and adults use wheelchairs,
But their minds are sharp and quick.
It's all right to offer your help,
But ask first or wait for the person to ask.
It should be the person's choice
To tell you if help is needed for a task.
Speak directly with a person who is disabled,
Rather than through someone nearby.
This makes the person feel more comfortable
And prevents his/her need to cry.

For a physically challenged person to get things done,
Appreciate what that person can do,
And you could find a friendship which has just begun.
Treat a person with a disability
The way you like to be treated.
Kind words and deeds are welcomed,
As well as smiles generously meted.
Invite the disabled person to your house
Or to join you in a place of interest that you like to go.
Think of ways to include him or her.
The result may be a happy face which will glow.
All persons who have disabilities
Should be given opportunities to "live, learn, work and play."
Then let us all understand and give a hand
That follows the traditions of the American way.

Part of this poem was inspired after reading the information provided
in the Easter Seals, 2009, request for funds: "Helpful hints for friends of
children who have disabilities."

OVERCOMING TOUGH TIMES

There are a number of reasons times are tough
For children near, far and wide:
Included are economics, exposure to material on
cyberspace or cell phones.
There is a lack of parental guidance by which children need to abide.
Children can learn bad stuff on the playground,
When they are visiting neighbors, or while on the street.
Many have unstable and lonely lives.
These children can be found at school, church,
camp— wherever one chances to meet.

There are ways to overcome the tough times.
First, one must be optimistic and be able to forgive.
When you can embrace a positive outlook,
Do accept hard times as a challenge— a more promising life to live.
Show respect for your father and mother,
Your school teacher, police, an office holder and friend.
Try to understand the other person's point of view.
When you act respectfully of others,
Others will come to respect you and the message you send.

The hard knocks received in life
Can often prepare one to accept victory or defeat.
Difficulties in life should not be a reason to quit.
So be determined, persistent, and refuse to cheat.
Don't be afraid to work hard in order to perform.
Though your days can be difficult and long,
You can lay a foundation for success.
Why, you can even become the President or an icon for a song!

Set your mind on what you want to do.
Accept the old cliche': "Hitch your wagon to a star."
Almost anything is possible when you are willing to work,
So study and work hard, and you can go far.

The above poem was written after reading the article: "What President
Obama Can Teach America's Kids" by Bill O'Reilly in the *PARADE,*
August 9, 2009, pages 14-xiii.

AN ABUSIVE RELATIONSHIP

If you're ever in an abusive relationship,
Run away as fast as you can.
It's better to run, share and tell
Than stay where there's an abusive woman or man.

Be aware of strangers who might stop in a car.
Don't accept their gift at any price.
Unless it's the police or an emergency vehicle,
Run, but get their tag number is good advice.

There are many ways one can be abused:
By being struck or burned, or by cruel expressions of word and deed.
Illicit or pre-marital sex are other means of abuse,
As well as exposure to illegal drugs, even
smoke from marijuana or other weed.

Actions that tear you down rather then build you up;
Such as, unkind and curse words or words of hate.
In these ways too you can be abused.
Avoid these evil perpetrators and find a better fate.

What should you do if you are in an abusive relationship?
Tell your teacher, guidance counselor, pastor or an adult friend.
And if it's not your parents, also tell them.
There are services that can punish and bring most abuses to an end.

There are social services, aid to children and much more.
The police will make an investigation should you dial 911.
Even if you call and hang up,
They might still come on the run.

Unfortunately, there are those who will take advantage of
Children or of those who are vulnerable or weak,
But you don't have to live in an abusive situation.
Seek lawful action: let the evil, their consequences reap.

CHILD ABUSE

If youth, parents, adults or teachers
Know of a child who is being abused,
Under Florida law, they are obligated to make a report.★
The state child abuse hot line number is the one to use.
Information about the situation will be asked.
It is not even necessary to give your name,
But there will be a Child Protective Investigation
To check and make a report in order to restrain.

Abuse is the result of patterns of behavior
Of the family, baby sitter, or friends nearby.
Though signs of injury may appear in time,
Unfortunately, sometimes a child will be badly hurt or die.
Parenting education may be lacking;
Factors might include financial stress, alcohol or substance abuse;

Or parents may not have the ability to manage a child.
Whatever the cause, don't think, "Reporting is of no use."
Most child fatalities are the result
Of inexperienced parents or a care giver,
Who might lack the skills or have a substance abuse problem.
Then look for children who are too silent, or have an obvious tremor.
Look for visible injuries that appear.
Ask, "How did it happen or who did this to you?"
Slap marks on the face, pinch or teeth marks should be reported—
As should bruises on shins or elbows that have turned blue.

Child protective services and the court system
In a crisis will place children with someone they know.
They'll work together to keep the child safe.
And preventative steps can be taken so
that the child can live and grow.

★If not in Florida, check for other numbers.

Information above was based on an article in *The Gainesville Sun,* Speaking
Out, by Ester Tibbs, Sunday, May 24, 2009. The Florida Abuse Hotline
Number is: 1-800-962-2873.

DEPRESSION

Depression is the emotion of feeling sad.
It may follow a recent loss or other unhappy event.
Depression can be common in adolescents.
Varying in degree with a problem of not being content.

Depression can be caused by the death of a parent.
It can be failure in adjusting to school,
Or the loss of a friend who has moved away,
Or problems in not following a new policy or rule.

Another reason may be difficulty in making close friends
And not being able to share as one intends.
Other causes of depression could be excessive drug or alcohol use.
These could all lead to suicidal tendencies from the abuse.

Suicidal behavior is a sign of mental illness—
Often sparked by a deep loss.
It could be the loss of familiar surroundings
or of a girl or boyfriend
Or conflicts with a parent or other "boss."

Depression can be caused by pressure to succeed,
Or a disciplinary experience might trigger an attempt of suicide.
It might be a "copy cat" action observed by that of others,
Trying to get attention from every side.

Don't think what you do will cause others to be sorry
In case you die or are dead.
Rather, remember that you can have a good life to live,
So seek counsel, psychological or medical
help— and have nothing to dread.

GREED

Each day that we live, we are planting seed:
Seeds of charity from our bounty or seeds of greed.
Seeds of kindness are shared in the neighborhood,
And that's what many have followed and understood.

Seeds of greed are selfish and bad.
Seeds of greed can make others angry, resentful or sad.
Greed is included in the Seven Deadly Sins.★
Then let's avoid the selfish trait and win some good friends.

Jail time often follows greed and other Deadly Sins,
Not only by our government but by our fellow men.
Other evils include lust, gluttony, wrath, envy and pride.
It's better to use the inverse virtues and from them not hide.

Virtues are charity, chastity, temperance, diligence,
Patience, kindness, humility, and loving care—
All of these attributes are good ones to follow;
These are all qualities— good and beyond compare.

Now when you find those who charge more than is proper,
And ask too much for a product they call a "whopper,"
Go elsewhere, because those who really want to succeed
Will support an honest deal and not support greed.

★The Roman Catholic Church recognizes Seven Virtues which
correspond inversely to each of the Seven Deadly Sins.

LOOK OUT FOR SCAMMERS

Economic times are often tough,
And the lives of many are consequently rough—
Unemployment, inflation, mortgage foreclosures and
rising cost of health care,
But we need to keep hope, but of scammers be aware.

With government stimulus and bail-out money flying around,
Government grant scams are frequently found.
Once the scammers receive your money for a processing fee,
You never hear from them again, and they're home free.

All of us want to have a good credit score.
For a flat fee, scammers order the victim's credit
report; and, there's more.
Negative items that they challenged and removed don't last long.
Once items are verified as accurate, they
reappear, but the scammers are long gone.

Another scam is cash-for-gold.
If we send in our broken jewelry or pieces that are old,
They will not pay what they're worth but send a
check for a whole lot less.
By then the items are melted and they're gone
with no returns— and no contest.

There are other scams, such as mystery shopping.
The scammer sends a cashier's check for a shopping spree that
will keep you hopping.
In no time, you find you have a fraudulent check,
And the money, if spent, could make your bank account a wreck.

"Online friendship" is another way scammers scam.
They say they're in jail, lost their car or home and
convince you they're in a jam.
They'll send a check to cash for them or they'll
just ask for money direct.
After it's too late, you've lost it all and there's no way to collect.

LOOK OUT FOR SCAMMERS
(CONTINUED)

Let's all think before we act or spend,
And be careful to whom we may lend.
If in doubt, call the Sheriff's office or the FBI about a crime.
Refuse to be a victim of scammers at any time.

The information for the above poem was gleaned from a talk given by Alachua County Sheriff Sadie Darnell to the North Florida Retirement Village residents on August 4, 2009. The contents might be a guide to older individuals.

GAMBLING

There are many venues to gambling,
As there are laws and policies to control these acts.
Gambling can also be very addictive,
So be aware of the snares and the facts.

Laws of the states have "simple" and "aggravated" gambling.
But there are penalties for misdemeanors and felonies too.
Some gambling statutes do not permit gambling on the Internet,
So if you should try your hand, know what might be taboo.

Some states receive much revenue from gambling;
To them, it is often of economic merit.
But it can lead to political corruption, compulsive
gambling and crime rates;
Therefore, gambling is not considered desirable —one bit.

Gambling may be broken down into gross revenues of sectors:
Commercial, casinos, lotteries, Indian Gaming,
Jai-alai, dog and horse.
There are also charitable games,
Card games, and Bingo, of course.

Some gambling is called gaming.
Some social gambling is allowed.
In Florida, $10.00 is the most
"Permitted" to be paid, the rule of game thus avowed.

Online sports betting Web sites are illegal.
Other forms of gambling on the Internet have not been resolved.
The validity and constitutionality of some statutes have not
been tested in the courts.
Even so, is it better not to become involved?

There are fights that are' hurtful, inhumane and harmful;
Such as, bull, rooster, and dog fights.
We are taught to be kind to animals
Stay away from these illegal and cruel gambling sites.

GAMBLING (CONTINUED)

If you should gamble, chances are that you will lose,
And losing may cause you to sing the "blues."
Refuse to be a gambler, as some teens are.
Remember most addictions have been difficult to break by far.

Invest your time and money in something
that brings you good returns.
Study, not gamble, and money you could save.
Never invest in anything more than you can lose.
Make good choices and not to gambling be a slave.

Even penny-ante games in a home are
illegal for those under eighteen.
Legally, a person cannot be charged admission to a game.
So if you want to stay on the road of doing what's right,
Remember taking bets will not enhance your good name

Information for this poem was gleaned from the Internet, from the Florida
Statutes, television, and from personal experiences with youngsters.

SAFE HAVENS FOR BABIES VS. ABANDONMENT

When my parents visited Cuba— prior to the Castro Days—
They were impressed
With how the Cubans took care of unwanted
babies in different ways.
If a mother could not take care of her baby,
She could leave it at a special place
Where it would be taken care of—with love and grace.

Since then, laws have been changed in the United States.
They have made it easier for all babies to live.
They can be dropped off at designated places,
Where they might have a chance to grow and give.
In Florida, there are Safe Havens for Newborns
At hospitals, ambulance and fire stations.
One can take a baby with complete anonymity:
Free from fear of prosecution or of other repercussions.

If you find that you are expecting a child
And you don't know what to do,
Go to a Crisis Pregnancy Center,
Where counseling, necessities and other help are offered to you.
If you should have thoughts of abandoning a child,
In a garbage can or along the highway,
Remember there are ways that you can be caught
And end up in jail for many a day.
This information is something we need to share:
By law all hospitals are required to offer care.
Now if you are not in the position of taking care of the child,
Surely, you want him or her to have a good life without guile.
If you've chosen life, go ahead and give birth to a little one
And consider offering the child up for adoption
To give him a chance for a place in the sun.

The poem above was written after reading the headlines and the article in *The Gainesville Sun* on Tuesday, June 2, 2009, regarding an abandoned baby found in a box on the side of an Ocala road. Lacy C. Lawrence, R.N., added to the accuracy and additional information in the poem.

LEARN GOOD THOUGHTS WHILE YOU'RE YOUNG

There are many sages' thoughts we might want to learn,
And when we are all alone, to us these words could return.
There are certain good thoughts we'll want to
keep always within our heart;
And then to others, these same words
we'll some day want to impart.

The melodious words and beautiful music that we learn
Will live on and to sing them again, we'll often yearn.
Then let's reflect on the good thoughts within
our hearts and minds,
And as we age, we'll be happy as we recall
those happy rhymes and lines.

Remember the example, "Two wrongs will never make a right,"
And "Everyone is precious in our legal system's sight."
Let us heed the teachings from then to now,
Our morals, ethics, and values thus endow.

Some other thoughts that might inspire and be a comfort in times of repose follow:

Only the disciplined are free. (James C. Penney)

Experience is not what happens to you; it is what you do with what happens to you. (Aldous Huxley)

Human beings, like chickens, thrive best when they have to scratch for what they get. (Harold Hayden)

A teacher is one who, in his youth, admired teachers. (H. L. Mencken)

Please all and you will please none. (Aesop)

After all there is but one race - humanity. (George Moore)

If a man loses reverence for any part of life, he will lose reverence for all of life. (Albert Schweitzer)

GOOD THOUGHTS TO LIVE BY

All of us have a god,
Whether we know it or not.
It's whatever we place first in our life.
It can be a Supreme Being, food, a job, politics,
A car, an animal, a house, a mate — all the money we've got.

Many believe there is a Spiritual Being
Whom we should not profane.
When laws and Commandments are obeyed in love,
Our words and deeds are rewarded; they're not in vain.

All of us need a time to rest.
It's good for our mind, body and soul.
We can worship, or have a change of pace.
Rest helps to make us more healthy, happy and whole.

Our mother and father deserve our respect—
No matter who they are or what they've done.
Even though they may have fallen short,
Resolve all wrongs before the setting of the sun.

When we're in war, we sometimes have a need to kill,
But it's evil to murder — even in our hearts.
Let's try to love and forgive each other—
Before our anger starts.

Let us take care of and respect our own body.
And when married not be promiscuous, and to our mate be true.
Let us respect the bodies which belong to others.
Avoid sexual transmitted diseases—a fate which we would rue.

All of us who work and save.
Want to keep or share as we choose:
We don't want to steal or have our property stolen.
Help is available for those in need, so stealing we should refuse.

GOOD THOUGHTS TO LIVE BY
(CONTINUED)

We have a Court system where a judge or jury
Can try to help make things right.
Let us be sure that we do not accuse anyone falsely,
But tell the truth and be a beacon of light.

If we work and save
But not strive just to keep up with our neighbor,
We will not want what someone else has;
We'll be proud of who we are and what we have,
Because it's from our own labor.

THE MEANINGS OF FAITH

"Faith is being sure of what we can hope for,
And it is also certain of things we do not see."
Faith is used in religion and medical science,
Even in placing trust in the effects of electricity.

Faith is having confidence in or dependence upon a person;
Faith can be in a statement or in words we sing;
Faith is belief without the need of certain proof;
But belief in what that faith hopes to bring.

By faith we do many things.
It's even by faith when we sit in a chair.
Although no one may be holding it,
When we sit, by faith we expect it to be there.

Often we go to a dentist or doctor
And report that we have pain.
Now pain is felt but cannot be seen,
But by faith, our doctors believe and relief we often gain.

It's by faith we open a bank account—
Or take out a money market or C. D.
It's by faith, we take out an insurance policy,
And it's by faith we count on our freedoms and liberty.

THE MEANINGS OF FAITH
(CONTINUED)

Although we cannot see the air we breathe,
We know that the air and wind are powerful and strong.
The air waves provide means for radio, TV and cell phones—
And health-wise, good, clean air is what we hope for and long.

Electricity is very much like the God in whom many believe.
It cannot be seen, but it's so full of power.
It's used all over the world
In households, offices and in traffic lights each day and hour.

DON'T GIVE UP

There are abused and neglected children.
There are those who have parents who do not seem to care.
But don't give up; there is a way out.
There are counselors and volunteers who
will prove that life can be fair.

Some children are in a home
Where there is a lifestyle of chronic drugs and alcoholic abuse.
But there are places where living conditions are safe.
Don't give up; there are foster and
Children's Homes available for use.

Some children are full of resentment and anger.
They don't like their teacher, other pupils, or anyone.
They can't forget the things that happened to them.
Don't give up; there are those who care and
will accept you as a daughter or son.

There are those who do not finish high school.
They fall in with and follow a gang on the street.
They end up doing things against the law,
But there are helpers with whom you need to meet.

There are many children who are victims.
Their situations would almost break your heart,
But there are volunteer adults who offer courage and confidence.
Don't give up; you can make a new start.

Now if you have been neglected or abused,
Or if you are an orphaned child,
Talk to your pastor, your teacher or counselor.
Don't give up; there are good places where
you might share a domicile.

DON'T GIVE UP (CONTINUED)

As you continue on your journey of life,
Think about where and what your inner self wants you to be.
Don't give up; but focus on things of value and hope.
You can find success and love in this world and society.

You might want to draw a picture illustrating a place in which
you would like to live.

INTRODUCTION TO "BOREDOM" (NEXT PAGE)

The reading and study of poems on "Boredom" could be divided into two sections or pages. Discussion in the first section apropos the subject of boredom, could be more meaningful with the display on maps of the area, parks, the museum, and historical sites mentioned in the poems. Follow-up could be an interpretation of their importance and function — the possible subject of oral or written reports.

Each poem in the second section on "Boredom" could be read, stanza by stanza, from which each student might select a subject of particular interest to him/her and find rewarding to do further study for a report. Subjects could lead to thoughts or discussions about future careers.

(There are many useful places for teens and others to visit and things to do in order to avoid boredom and thus avoid getting into trouble).

BOREDOM

There are teens and others who find life boring
And don't know what to do,
So they become troublemakers in malls and stores,
Dressing like a chicken, a banana, and even a gingerbread man too.

The teens gleefully record their shenanigans
And post them on You Tube or sites; such as, MySpace.
They make videos and use cell phone cameras.
They think it's fun to give store managers a wry face.

Other teens go through a neighborhood.
They break windows and enter cars.
They steal items that they find
And even go into open bars.

Some teens break into school houses
Where they abuse property and then destroy.
They steal or break the latest equipment.
Destructive acts, they seem to enjoy.

Thankfully, all teens have not gone astray.
They fmd constructive things to do.
They volunteer for community service like Habitat for Humanity.
As a volunteer, they help, not hurt others— the latter action to rue.

There are many opportunities for service.
That will help teens stay out of jail.
They should learn that half of success is a try
And learn ways to repeat, "Never say fail."

Teens don't need to be bored.
They can plant seeds, start a garden, or go fishing.
There is always something they can find to do,
But they should know when they need to ask for permission.

BOREDOM (CONTINUED)

State parks and camp grounds
Can offer outdoor family fun,
Where they can see alligators, wild horses, bison,
And other wildlife on the run.

Some state parks and campgrounds have
Nature trails, bike trails, kayaks and canoe.
Picnic tables are also available
Where families can enjoy a barbeque.

To visit state parks and campgrounds,
There are small charges visitors would need to pay.
Zoos, museums, parks, and historic sites also
Are all great places to keep boredom away.

Hiking can be great fun.

BOREDOM (CONTINUED)

Teens can think of many things
That they can write or say.
They can compose music or author songs
That will help brighten someone else's day.

Teens can always practice games or sports,
Take a hike or ride a bike in the woods or along a safe highway.
They can play checkers or a game of chess or
work crossword puzzles.
Also, many churches and synagogues are open, where teens
can play ball, worship and pray.

There are usually workshops and craft shows
That teens can register to attend.
Several activities can lead to a vocation.
They can even enter contests and win.

Teens can become good photographers,
And take pretty pictures along the way.
Often photos can be developed and sold
As works of art or be hung in a café.

There is always a demand for good food,
And everyone can learn to become a good cook.
Different classes and courses are offered.
Options such as gourmet, they should not overlook.

Teens can learn how to swim, go boating, skiing or surfing,
But they should go where there are life guards at the beach or pool.
In Florida there are lots of water holes and springs,
But they should be careful and not play the fool.

In some places, teens can "shadow" a business.
They can ride on a fire truck or in a police car.
They can observe a trial by jury,
Listen to a concert or learn to play and sing with a guitar.

BOREDOM (CONTINUED)

Drama, dance and acting appeal to many teens.
Communication is often a good way to go.
Teens might have a chance to be on television or on the radio,
But to profane dialogue or lyrics a teen should say, "NO!"

Having learned to read, teens could look for books,
Which they can check out and spend time reading each day.
They can study in the school libraries—and in the public
ones which are there for all.
The media specialist is there to help them find their way.

Teens should try to take part in activities that are free of crime.
They should not fight, rob, kidnap, rape or steal.
They should avoid smoking tobacco, marijuana or drinking alcohol
And refrain from riding with an intoxicated
person behind the wheel.

Before college, teens can start their own business.
They can wash cars or sell lemonade,
But they should check to see if they need a license
Before they start their own trade.

Other ways of helping out
Would be to rake yards or mow,
Clean houses or wash clothes and iron,
Or pull weeds from a garden row.

Teens should learn how to save and make use
of the credit union or bank.
By all means, they should open a savings account.
They never know of opportunities that might occur,
And savings could add up to a substantial amount.

It is never too early for teens to start thinking and studying
About what they want to do when they complete high school.
They can read and learn about the different colleges
And then apply early to register and follow each prescribed rule.

BOREDOM (CONTINUED)

Teens can learn about scholarships,
As they study and do their best each day and on each test.
The different colleges offer scholarships with financial aid,
And their teachers, pastors and adult friends
will listen and procedures suggest.

Teens should be honest and truthful to their God and themselves,
Wherever they happen to be.
They don't have to be bored with so many good things to do.
They can have a happy, busy and successful
life in this land of the free.

Teens should study and do their best each day.

AS YOU BECOME A MAN OR WOMAN

Now that you are becoming a man or a woman,
You have passions and feelings known to every race and clan.
You can either let your feelings get out of control
Or think before you act and know that you have a plan.

Although cultures, traditions, values and standards
Seem to change and evolve through the years,
It is up to each one to make decisions and choices
That will bring either joy or heartaches and tears.

At one time, a man and woman lived together
Only after marriage had taken place.
This is still a more desirable option
And is more acceptable in some cultures and race.

There are many attractions and temptations
That can often get in one's way.
Television and adult magazines get out of line
And offer sex and pornography for a brighter day.

There are brothels and prostitution rings
That solicit sex for those passing by.
They are an illegal business and you can be arrested,
So keep on driving or walking, and that business do not try.

There are times that drugs and alcohol
Will cause individuals to perform acts and do wrong things.
It's better to say, "NO" and not get involved;
Refrain from steps that an inadvertent action often brings.

It's really better to wait until marriage,
Before you actively engage in sex;
Because if you let your desires and passions get out of control,
Your life becomes more complex.

AS YOU BECOME A MAN OR WOMAN (CONTINUED)

Now if you have already violated this advice,
And you have previously gone astray,
It is good to be checked by a doctor
To make sure that you and your health are doing 0. K.

Get to know your partner and his/her family background,
Because there are many sexually transmitted diseases,
And if you should have more than one partner,
You are risking your health and a remorse that never ceases.

If babies are conceived without benefit of marriage,
There are decisions you will need to make.
First, are you old enough, and do you want to
marry the father or mother
To give your child a good name and one
whom you'll not ever forsake?

There's a basis for your decisions
And a freedom in what you believe, say and do.
Your morals, ethical and religious thinking come into play:
Faith in your God, your parents, your clergy and
then your pro-choice or pro-life avenue.

It takes a lot of time, love, attention and expense
To take care of any child.
Although the child was conceived in illicit sex,
Surely, you don't want your offspring to grow up to be wild.

Make sure you have someone who will take care
Of your child when he/she arrives.
You'll need clothes, diapers, milk and much more.
Confide in your parents to make sure that your child thrives.

AS YOU BECOME A MAN OR WOMAN (CONTINUED)

Although sex was consensual in what the mother might have done,
Remember that she is still in control.
Even if a pregnancy was by rape or by force,
She is now in charge of her body, mind and soul.

If all else fails, another option is a legal abortion,
And many consider this as the way,
But when an unborn child is aborted or murdered,
The mother, emotionally and psychologically, may have to pay.

Before you ever consider an abortion procedure,
Get the best possible spiritual, medical and psychological advice.
You might experience a feeling of guilt and a life of regret,
Because the mother and child in the mother's womb pay a price.

Now if you have already taken this step,
And have cried your eyes out night and day,
Ask for forgiveness of your family and your God,
And start a purpose-filled and guided life after you pray.

Let others not be too quick to judge
Those who have let their passions get out of control.
They have to live with their mistakes and decisions.
Help them make a life for themselves as they try to become whole.

Whatever is decided involves many others:
Your partner, both sets of parents, family members, your school,
community and your God.
It is better not to have to live a life of regret,
So live and try to be guilt-free on the road you have
chosen to trod.

AS YOU BECOME A MAN OR WOMAN (CONTINUED)

Yes, it's much better to wait to have sex,
Until you find someone with whom you wish to
spend the rest of your days.
After you get your education and then a good job,
You can act responsibly and thus receive much deserved praise.

This poem was written after reading and listening to the news, having a stimulating conversation with a friend, and observing the lives of young people as they live and struggle in today's society.

YOU HAVE FREE WILL

You have been given free will to hopefully choose
And make wise decisions on your own.
But you need to choose thoughtfully and wisely;
So that a life of good seed you will have sown.

From twelve to seventeen years of age,
Youth are rarely equipped or ready to be thinking of marriage.
Some enter into a relationship based on emotions and feelings
That frequently lead to sex, followed by
an abortion or a baby carriage.

Teens are not psychologically prepared to become a parent.
To suffer the consequences can dramatically alter one's life.
Failure to observe the caution and stop signs
Can lead to an unhappy life that is filled with strife.

Dating is usually sharing a friendship with
someone of the opposite sex
That leads to finding a partner for life and in building a home.
Then don't rush into the dating game.
It is better to wait until you are more
mature and are full grown.

Also, it is best to be equally yoked together.
A sound spiritual relationship will help survive
the storms that come.
Selecting the appropriate person whom you marry
Can help you along the right path you've hopefully begun.

REMEMBER TO SAY "THANK-YOU"

If someone invites you for an evening of fun,
Soon after enjoying the event.(a movie, bowling, or a time to dine),
Write them or call them to say, "Thank you."
Let them know that you had a very good time.

If there are those who care enough
To send you a card, or a gift, or offer you a job for pay,
Remember to say, "Thank-you,"
And wish them a happy and good day.

If someone helps you with your housework or a physical need,
No matter how limited you are to respond in the situation,
Still let them know how you feel;
Give them a smile and a thank-you in appreciation.

Grandparents, parents, aunts and uncles are sometimes forgotten.
Youngsters often think that their relations are "supposed" to give.
Although they have worked and saved and may want to help,
They do like to be shown appreciation for as long as they live.

If someone gives you a gift,
Thank them in word and deed.
A written note is frequently cherished,
And good manners will help you be accepted and succeed.

WHO ARE WE?

Do we have faith and do good works?
Do our works prove what we believe?
Are we hearers or are we doers?
Does our lifestyle support us or does it deceive?

If we have faith and do good works,
Other people we will serve.
Also, we'll want to show love for God and country,
And not keep our doing and acting in reserve.

Our faith and obedience are demonstrated in loving service.
It's up to us to decide how, when and where we serve.
It may look different at various stages of life,
But let's always do what's right and not ever lose our nerve.

If we are making a name for ourselves,
Others will come to know us for what they see.
If we study, work and practice our faith in love,
We will be "Doers" who would be free.

The above poem was inspired by "Live Your Faith" by writer Polly Cooper Brown, a retired psychologist who lives in Huntsville, Texas.

GIVERS AND TAKERS - MOVERS AND SHAKERS

There are givers and takers around us.
Which one do you want to be?
Do you take all you can get?
Is giving nothing in return your recipe?

There are also movers and shakers
Who work hard to get things done.
They include others to help with their mission.
When people help each other, working together is fun.

Then there are those who are self-centered and selfish.
They want to do nothing to better themselves at all.
If others reinforce their laziness and selfishness,
Are they not being set-up for a great fall?

There are times it's better to say no
When others manipulate in an effort to get their own way.
Let's wish for the wisdom and courage
To do what is right in helping, or not helping, each day.

There is a time to be a giver or a mover and shaker.
And there is a time to be a taker, too.
But the more that you do to help yourself and then
give service to others
Will bring satisfaction and a feeling of contentment to you.

WHEN YOU'RE INVITED
OUT TO DINE

When you're invited out to dine,
Water, milk, juice or tea should be fine.
Then order fish, chicken or turkey as your meat,
And remember to sit up straight in your seat.
Cut your food as you eat each bite.
Learning good manners will help you do what's right.
Fruit and vegetables are good for you.
Place your napkin in your lap, but leave it unfolded
when you're through.
Go slow on desserts, pastas and bread.
Obesity then, should never be something you'll need to dread.
Remember to say: "Thank you," "Excuse me," and "Please."
And use a handkerchief or Kleenex if you should cough or sneeze.
While dining, leave your hair and face alone,
And refuse to talk on your cell phone.
Keep your voice and laughter low so that you don't disturb;
Then other guests will think your manners are superb.
Keep table conversation pleasant and sweet;
And a happy get-together, while dining, will be more complete.
Now although your name may not be Mable,
Remember to keep your elbows off the table.

IF YOU ARE ENSLAVED

If you have an addiction and have become enslaved
Because of poor choices that you've made along the way,
It's important to know that there is a way out.
You, however, must <u>want</u> to be delivered from your problem today.
There are times you need to stop and think
Before you buy or take things you don't need.
With the right choices you can avoid
The path to destruction or greed.

Always seek freedom from your bondage;
The goal is to gain a victory each night and day.
Then try to understand your psychological needs involved.
Search for guidance and good counsel along life's highway.
Whatever your bondage, you can be set free.
You have been given free will to choose.
If your problem is drugs, drinking, smoking, gluttony or sex,
When you are <u>ready</u> to stop, with help from
a higher power, you'll not lose.

The same freewill that led you to drink, gamble or smoke,
Or whatever your bondage might be,
That same freewill, if rightly exercised,
Will help you win a victory.

Once again you can experience
True joy, peace and abundance in this life.
You can find freedom from your enslavement
And have strength to live a happy life—
free of addiction and strife.

The above poem was based on a devotional received via E-mail
from Bill Keller on October 31, 2009.

THANKS TO OUR TROOPS - PAST AND PRESENT

Our troops "over there" are defending our future,
As we at home celebrate America's past.
The Army, Air Force, Navy, Marines and Coast Guard
Are spread over the globe fighting for our
freedoms, which we pray will last.

As politics and the economy dominate the nightly news,
Let's not forget the brave men and women who are giving their all;
They're putting their lives on the line:
To defend America, they answered their country's call.

As we enjoy our backyard cookouts and picnics,
Or play or watch softball or attend a parade,
As we "ooh" and "ah" at fireworks displays,
Some of our troops are ducking live rounds
of a rocket-propelled grenade.

They and those who have served in the past are our stars and heroes.
We thank them and those who are now fighting for our
freedoms— to defeat the terrorists and foes.
All of us long for peace in our hearts and in our land,
Then let us study and follow our Constitution and
Amendments and give our
military personnel support by taking a stand.

The poem above was inspired after reading a letter requesting funds for the USO.

REFUSE TO BE IN A CLIQUE

At times there are groups called cliques.
They often unite and become a clan.
Membership (in the cliques) is often influenced by educational
class or social ranks,
And a self-importance seems to be their plan.

They may exclude others who have creative ability,
knowledge and charm.
Because they form a sophisticated company of
people with similar tastes,
They think that they themselves are better than others,
And narrowing isolation soon becomes their fates.

It is far better to avoid becoming clannish.
Reach out to everyone around.
But use good judgment and choose your friends wisely,
And success, self-respect and happiness may be found.

WHEN YOU SPEAK

When you speak, say what you mean
And mean what you say.
Avoid speaking against yourself
Or gossiping about others in any way.
Always speak with integrity.
Use the power of your word so true.
Take the direction of goodness and love
So that you'll never regret what you say or do.

Pay no attention to what others say.
Nothing others do or say is because of you.
It could be a protector of their own
insecurities and personalities.
Then be immune to the opinions and actions of others—
An unnecessary venue you need not pursue.

Find the courage to ask questions.
Seek answers before you have your say.
Communicate as clearly as you can to avoid misunderstandings,
Thus, you can transform your life in many a way.

Try to do your best in all you write, say and do,
Depending on whether or not you are healthy or ill.
Try to avoid self-judgment, self-abuse and regret,
And seek love, peace and good-will.

The poem above was inspired after reading "The Four Agreements"
(don Miguel Ruiz). 1. Be Impeccable with Your Word; 2. Don't
Take Anything Personally; 3. Don't Make Assumptions; and 4.
Always Do Your Best.

WREN THERE ARE
BAD ECONOMIC TIMES

When there are bad economic times,
It's time to put away your pride.
Face your feelings and emotions,
But from the truth, do not hide.
You may have worked up to the top
And were fired or let go to "reduce personnel."
Future employment depends upon your attitude
And your willingness to accept work beneath that in
which you have excelled.
You need to have a place to live and food to eat,
And if you don't want to move to the street
And live a homeless life,
Get up early each morning and do not accept defeat.

There are times that a job is a job.
Regardless of how little or how much pay you receive,
Do what you can to contribute to your family.
Keep your mind and body active, have trust and believe.
If it means mowing laws, working as a news carrier or at a fast food,
Waiting tables or shelving food at a grocery store,
Thus you can maintain your self-esteem,
But stay active until you can earn more.

There are times volunteer work can lead to a job.
It's important that you strive every day.
When others recognize your willingness to serve and give,
You might even be given a nice tip or pay.
It would be helpful to make a daily schedule,
And be flexible as you seek a job.
Be worthy of support as you take care of yourself.
Your self-respect, do not rob.

The above poem was inspired while watching the Dr. Phil show
on TV, Channel 4, on November 10, 2009,

SCHOOL UNIFORMS

A girl came to school wearing a shirt with wording on it.
She did not know what the words meant,
So to the office to wait her turn, she was sent to sit
Until the principal could talk to her, hear her reasons,
and then comment.
When the principal asked about the shirt,
She said that her mother's boyfriend dared her to wear it to school.
He wanted to know how the school personnel would react
And to see if she had broken a school rule.

This fourth grader said her school manual and
policies were on a shelf,
Which stated: "Be clean, neat and do not wear anything to
draw attention to one's self."
Her shirt and other shirts had words on them that were in poor
taste— almost obscene.
A different kind of shirt was needed on the school scene.

With this shirt and others with inappropriate words,
And for those students who wanted to act like nerds,
The board of instruction decided to correct
that behavior gone astray.
They passed a uniform code for students' attire each day.

Some of the pupils may not like the dress code that has come about,
But they will all need to conform, in case there is any doubt.
They can all wear their uniforms with pride,
And develop school spirit and learn much that the
teachers' classes provide.
No longer will the students need to spend time
wondering what to wear.
No longer will the students' choice of clothing be a statement
or a response to a dare.

SCHOOL UNIFORMS (CONTINUED)

Instead of their fighting the policy that has been passed,
They could try wearing a spirit of love, joy and peace that could last.
There is no law against acquiring these traits
Or to find one above these that rates.
They can spend their time on work and study in order to succeed;
And on the side, they might find time to
help others by doing a good deed.

REFUSE TO BE A SCHOOL DROPOUT

Refuse to be a school drop out.
If you don't listen, you could pay a terrible price.
If you stay in school, you can earn a better living,
And I trust that if you will accept this advice,
You can make an honest livelihood.
You can earn your own way.
You can give back to your family and country.
And you'll be glad that you stayed in school each day.

The high school drop outs average thirty percent.
Many youth join street gangs or go into drugs or crime.
They break the hearts of those who love them,
So stay in school; do what's right while young and in your prime.
Now, after you complete high school,
It would be good for you to go on to college.
Define the things you like to do,
Then study and gain more vocational and academic knowledge.

Most of us know of the beverage, Gatorade;
It was concocted at the U. F. by Doctor Robert Cade. ★
Doctor Cade was a high school drop out, because he was bored;
But he took and passed the GRE, went to college
and made a high grade.
Now, if you have already dropped out of school,
It's never too late to try again.
You can take the GRE more than once;
Pass it and apply for a scholarship; you could succeed and win.

★Dr. Robert Cade was a medical doctor at the University of Florida.

WHEN SEEKING A JOB

When you are looking for a job,
Use good manners, not those of a mob.
Others are looking for employment too,
So be patient and kind in what you say or do.

Don clothing that is appropriate for you to wear.
Be clean and neat from your feet to your hair.
Call for an appointment and then keep your schedule:
Arriving a little early is a very good rule.

When you are called in for your interview.
Looking the interviewer in the eye is a good avenue.
Have a well-prepared and neat resume' in your hand
That shows your strengths, your skills, crafts, typing or shorthand.

Ask questions about what you need to know.
Explain what you can do for them and how you
might chance to grow.
Let the interviewer know of your life's goals ahead.
Speak clearly and distinctly and you'll have nothing to dread.

Be sure to thank the interviewer for the time that was spent
And, hopefully, you'll get the job; then be
responsible for paying your rent.
There is usually a time-line that you may expect to hear.
So good luck in seeking a job; have no fear.

PLAN YOUR ESTATE

Everyone needs an estate plan—
If you are owners of property, small or large.
Or if you're the head of a household and its care,
Seek assistance and pay an attorney's charge.

If there are children, they could be assigned
To a guardian by the Court, unless you draft a will
That names the guardian of your choice.
If not, your wishes they will not fulfill.

If you don't have an estate plan,
Your estate will be distributed in accordance with the
law of the state.
It does not matter what your desires may be,
So take care of your legal work: do not leave it to fate.

Think about a charitable deduction.
It could benefit and achieve tax savings for you and your clan.
Just don't let too much time pass by
Before you complete your estate plan.

WORSHIP IS A LIFE'S DEEPEST NEED

Do we know who or what it is we place first in our lives?
It is the thing or person to whom we give the most zeal.
Worship is said to be one of life's deepest needs.
Dependence upon our God is real.

Most persons have a need for communion with God.
This longing is satisfied through worship, music and prayer.
Attendance in worship, reading the Bible,
saying grace before meals—
Can help provide us and our family tranquility,
comfort, security and care.

As a way of promoting God's way and will,
Denominations were organized for all and
were created by humankind.
Abraham was the father of the major denominations
And a study of Judaism, Christianity, Islam,
and/or others can help Seekers find.

Many believe there is only one true God,
About whom most of us can boast.
We can place our faith, hope and trust in Him—
The Trinity: the Father, the Son and Holy Ghost.

We should keep seeking until we find our way,
And find the God to whom we wish to pray.
We can hope to find peace and comfort from without and within,
And with joy and happiness, peace we can win.

HAVE YOU EVER TRIED TO WRITE?

Have you ever tried to write
About the story of your life?
Have you ever tried to tell about
The abounding joys and loves you found
As a child, or as a husband or wife?

I hope that when you and I have finished,
You will want to try writing a book.
You start with paper, pen, typewriter or computer
And find yourself a quiet nook.

If you get up early in the morning
When all is peaceful and quiet,
You'll find that writing is good therapy—
And it can be fun, so try it.

You can recall the days when you were young—
Before and after you started to school.
You can write a history of your life—
Even how you worked to change a law or rule.

You can tell of the things that made you happy,
But include the events that made you sad.
You can tell how you came to accept your God
And how He made your heart glad.

You can tell about your vocation or career.
Or share how on each job you were hired.
Disclose anecdotes you experienced there—
Even the incident or the time you were fired.

Tell how you met your spouse
And how he or she changed your life.
Tell of your siblings or children
Or about your grandchildren's husband or wife.

HAVE YOU EVER TRIED TO WRITE?
(CONTINUED)

Tell about a special vacation
And how glad you were to arrive back home.
Tell about flying, hiking, or driving,
Or a decision you made never again to roam.

You can start by writing a short story—
Then share it in your class, a seminar, workshop or group.
You'll find that creative writing is more lasting
Than working in a garden or making soup.

The poem above was first written for "The Silver Saints," Keystone Heights, Florida, January 16, 2003, but it has been modified for this book.

LIFE AND DEATH

Life and death come to all of us.
They do not pass us by.
It depends upon how we have lived:
Whether we laugh with joy or have a need to cry.

When we lose friends we dearly love,
Or family members who are close to us,
We can place our trust in an all-knowing God,
Light candles, send cards, take food,
make calls or offer condolences.

Tragedies often take place
In unexpected ways.
Funerals or memorials are usually scheduled
As a time to remember the lost one and to offer praise.

It's also a time to examine our own lives
And see what we might need to change.
We can visit our counselor, principal or pastor,
Because this spiritual journey may seem uncertain and strange.

This might be a time for additional study
To reach out and find a spiritual love that is real.
We can visit our church, synagogue or mosque
And pray that the truth they will reveal.

We can soon dry our eyes over our loss
And try to continue living a good life each day.
We can recall many things about our loved one
And remember their families— when and if we pray.

Hopefully, we'll all find joy, peace and hope
And a love and faith that will forever endure.
Then let's reach out to our family and neighbors
And live a good life that is purpose-filled and pure.

TO OUR YOUTH

This book of poems was written for you.
It tells of things that you might say or do.
It's a guide in ways to help you succeed,
But only if you will listen and take heed.

This book is one I trust will inspire
You to lead a good life— hopefully, that's the one you desire.
You must make good choices along the way.
Listen to parents, ministers and teachers in what they say.

I hope this book will be your guide,
And you'll find its secrets somewhere inside.
I trust that your life will be trouble and drug free
And that you'll stay in school— not an absentee.

Work and study hard in all you do
And be punctual, kind and honest too.
Refrain from stealing, for that is wrong.
Learn to express yourself in art, word or song.

Learn to use the computer and record your notes.
Or make a record of your favorite quotes.
If there are poems or passages you like and don't want to forget,
Arrange them to music and you could have a great outlet.

You might even decide to write your own book—
Include a short story or debate a subject about your outlook.
Tell about your life in a one or two-act play;
Or put words to music in your own special way.

I hope each reader will be a rising star
And will find happiness in life— whoever you are.
Being true to yourself is a must,
And it's your choice in whom you place your trust.

WHEN I TAUGHT

(This little poem expresses some of my beliefs and philosophy in teaching).

— Margaret A. Rosenberger

Some folks say that our youth have "gone bad" in our land.
If this is true, what have we done in giving a helping hand?
It is not too late to turn about face,
And do all that we can to help the human race.

When I taught, I encouraged the parents to volunteer:
To help their children at home and school all year.
We needed their partnership in education
In order to have the best instruction in the nation.
I suggested to parents to have someone at home after school
To welcome their children and be sure that they knew each rule.
They could give them a snack or two before the end of the day,
Then guide them to do their homework after their play.

When I taught, in social studies, I tried to teach that policies,
rules, and laws were made to obey;
But if citizens did not approve, to go through channels
And work for change in a non-violent and peaceful way.

My students were taught to have faith, love and hope,
And to stay off illegal drugs, tobacco, alcohol and dope.
I tried to teach youth to report, laugh at, or ignore some things;
Such as, name calling, profanity and offensive words
that an ill-chosen word often brings.

I tried to teach my pupils to be a true and loyal friend,
If they seek happiness that will never ever end.

WHEN I TAUGHT (CONTINUED)

My pupils were taught to say, "Thank you,"
"Excuse me," and "Please,"
For in the development of good manners,
they would feel more at ease.

I tried to show by example how to be firm but kind,
And that when they are honest and true, their likes they can find.
I tried to teach pupils to seek companions who were "for real,"
And not those who were found to cheat, lie or steal.

They should try to help those who have lost their way
By counseling, talking and taking time to pray.
I tried to teach children to stand on their own two feet.
Listen to all sides before accepting a win or admitting defeat.
I tried to challenge them to be diligent in work, study and play
And to read a good book each and every day.

My pupils were taught that nothing is really free.
Those benefits are provided from the payment
of taxes by you and me.
They were taught to respect property and their bodies as well
And to get up and start all over, if they ever fell.

I tried to teach our youth to love their fellow-man,
And even though he is different, try to respect and understand.
I tried to teach them to ignore some things;
Look at the flowers and listen to the bird that sings.
I encouraged our youth to strive to do their best,
For the time would come when their abilities and
education would be put to a test.
I so wanted our youth to have good-will and peace
And love for themselves and others that would never ever cease.
I suggested that the pupils report any child abuse;
To seek spiritual counseling and guidance and put it to good use.
For it is better to choose a good name
Than to have riches with a questionable reputation and fame.

A WORD TO PARENTS

A great responsibility is mother and fatherhood,
So love your children as you should.
Teach your children right from wrong.
Teach them good words to music and song.
Make sure that your children get to school on time.
When they're in school, there's no time for crime.
The teachers have the right to correct your child,
'Cause they act in your place for a little while.
Support the teachers when your child is in school,
But hear all sides is a very good rule.
Have your children do their homework before going to bed,
Then they can face the school day with nothing to dread.
Require your child to sit and eat.
Good food and conversation can be a treat.
Read books and teach good manners as a way to act.
Then thoughtful and good citizenship will be intact.
Teach your children to stay off of the street.
That's no place for good friends to meet.
Now, if they should happen to fall and are found guilty one night.
Let them take their punishment, for this is right.
There are times "tough love" is the only way
To keep your children from going astray.

REFLECTIONS ON REARING CHILDREN

Parents, your values are important today.
Your influence instills qualities in your children in every way.
They first learn what's right and wrong from you
And then from others they love, respect and admire too.

Your actions speak louder than what you say.
Your children observe you, your honesty and respect
for self and others each day.
Parents have the important task of child-rearing.
They should create an environment full of caring—
One that will teach them a loving and caring respect for
themselves and others.
You do have a tough job to teach your children
to be loving sisters and brothers.

Emotions can often run very high,
Especially when they become teens and your patience, they try.
They may check out the values of their peers
And try out drugs and alcohol that could cause your tears.
Such entanglements can ruin their life,
Destroy their earliest ambitions and bring all much strife.

If teenagers don't get what they need at home,
They may run away from pressure and decide to roam.
The stakes are high: your child could drop out of school
Or become a pregnant teenager — a fate most cruel.

Parents, please have patience, faith, love and hope.
Set an example for your children
And stay off of drugs, tobacco, marijuana, alcohol and dope.

PARENTS, THEIR CHILDREN AND VICE

Parents should take care of their children physically and spiritually.
Oh, if only all parents would adhere to this advice!
Surely, they don't want their child to become addicted!
Lead them to be mature and good citizens who are free of vice.

Parents need to be aware and alert
To the problems of underage drinking.
Children and teenagers should be teetotalers.
Parents need to watch for any trouble in the making!

Parents are often surprised
To learn that their youth and teenagers
Know where alcohol and drugs can be found.
When parents aren't home, some children
drink and even take wagers.

The "latch-key kids" really need supervision
When they are looking for fun.
They don't need to get alcohol from the refrig
Or from friends or other adults who are over twenty-one.

The Federal Trade Commission
Has campaigns against underage drinking.
Since April is Alcohol Awareness Month,
Parents should talk to their children and clarify their thinking.

Parents can get information on the Web.
To help with a general discussion.
They can study and talk to their child:
They can make a difference without commotion.

Surely, parents don't want to lose their teenagers
In an accident caused by D-W-I.
Then let's help to make our homes and streets safer;
So that fewer parents or youth will need to cry or die.

AFTER THE SUPREME COURT RULING
(THE OTHER SIDE)

In the 1960s the Supreme Court ruled
That there must be separation of church and state.
Bibles and prayers were taken out of schools;
Then drugs, guns and violence became our fate.

About that time, desegregation became the law.
Bussing had to take place to integrate.
This caused upsets and heartaches
And mixed feelings of love and hate.

Some public school educators are afraid to mention God
And the way our forefathers planted seed.
Now God is mentioned only in the pledge,
Though the Bible was the Book by which
they were taught to read.

Pupils were to learn how to read the Scripture,
Because it is the Holy Book.
Never in the wildest dreams of our forefathers
Could they realize that their vision would be forsook.

Peoples of all races must work together.
They can also join together in school, worship and song.
Though cultures are different, we can still co-exist,
And through love, may we find a peace and
a place in which all can belong.

Except for the last verse, the above poem was first published on page
145 of *The Other Side Where Love Knows No Color (Secrets and Songs)* by
Margaret A. Rosenberger, 2006, Rose Hill Publications.

HOW THINGS HAVE CHANGED

I loved to hear the stories our grandmothers shared with me
About the tales their grandma told when they were twenty-three.
Except for the native Indians,
There were legal immigrants in this land.
They loved this country, that is true,
and at Gettysburg, Pennsylvania,
They made a statement; they took a stand.

Transportation was by horse and carriage, a wagon, ship or train.
Homes were log cabin, brick, shot-gun or frame.
Heat was by a fireplace or a pot-bellied stove.
Most had gardens in their backyards and/
or an orange tree or a grove.
White clothing was boiled in a big black pot in the back yard,
Soap was made with lye and the well-water was hard.
Baths were taken only once a week.
There were no deodorants which we now seek.
There was always a little house out back,
Because electricity, running water and in-
door bathrooms they did lack.
Mail was by sea, pony express, or telegraph.
They had no telephones, TVs, computers,
Blackberries, I-Pods or a mimeograph.
After homes, churches were built, so that
God's Commandments would guide.
Cemeteries were next to the churches in the countryside.
The schools were first begun for the pupils to learn to read.
The Holy Bible was their text book with
instructions for their every need.
They learned to write with chalk and slate.
They had to work hard, focus and concentrate.
All the pupils went to school in a one room.
Romance often bloomed and life-long marriages occurred soon.

HOW THINGS HAVE CHANGED
(CONTINUED)

Today, no longer can Bibles be read or prayers be
said in the public schools,
Because that would be violating a Supreme Court decision that rules.
We now have profanity, violence, gangs, drugs and guns.
Since Bibles were taken out, good attitudes, good
manners and polite courtesy, a pupil often shuns.

In my grandmother's time, the wedding vows were
between one man and one woman to marry.
It's now legal in some states for it to be between
James and Harry and Jane to Carrie.

The definitions or usage of words no longer mean the same.
They go far beyond a crossword puzzle game.
For everything, there was a right or wrong.
No longer is it appropriate to say, "Be happy and gay,"
Because it can be taken in the wrong way.
My grandmother was taught to be proper—and somewhat prim.
She could not say "leg;" it had to be "a lower limb."
Grandma would never listen to or tell an off-colored joke,
And she had never heard of or seen a woman
who would drink or smoke.

Now our grandmother was a "modest beauty,"
Any place she chanced to go.
Her long golden hair upon her head
Framed her face and formed a crowning glow.
She wore long sweeping dresses (with a hat).
It was not proper for her to cross her knees.
She always wore her gloves and took her hankie—
Just in case she had to cough or sneeze.

Now when the girls wanted to go for a swim,
They wore long black stockings and full attire.

HOW THINGS HAVE CHANGED
(CONTINUED)

But if they dared get wet and a man wanted to exercise with them,
He was delegated to the shore, but his
glimpses of them would never tire.

Then with her sweetheart, soft glimpses were exchanged.
Their wedding plans would soon be arranged.
Murmured sighs were soft and sweet.
No physical display.
They spoke of love with their eyes— no need to speak

When a lady admired an eligible fellow in America's earlier days,
For him, she would "set her bonnet" to
capture his attention and gaze.

But now, how things have changed the way girls attract!
Could this be a part of the generation gap?
Would our ancestors with high standards of conduct be full of alarm?
Or would they call this flagrant pursuit a disgrace or charm?

We know women now paint their nails, their lips and face.
They try to outdo each other in the fashion race.
Some wear a bikini, short-shorts and skimpy wraps.
Instead of "setting their bonnet" as they did long ago,
Some girls now think it's cool to allure with their "knee caps."

Mores, standards and values in the olden days
Were good and sound in many ways.
Let's study and learn from them as we grow,
And the Supreme Being and you yourself, you might come to know.

TIME FLIES

Time flies when we're having fun,
Regardless of our age or place.
Fond childhood memories remain for most of us,
But for others, that's not the case.

When a mother or father is an alcoholic or on drugs,
Or if there is no money for food or clothes,
The children can feel trapped, afraid and angry,
And steal or sell drugs for their unhappy state and woes.

Rather than going astray, let us take time to relish each moment,
Recalling all the good things that have come into play.
Should there be a problem within our home,
Let's seek resources and guidance to keep bad behavior at bay.

There are ways to grow into better men and women,
But we must make each day count by doing our best—
With dedication and commitment, like volunteers
Who have love and from service never rest.

With understanding, wisdom, knowledge and a good education,
Time well-used can fly as we mature.
Through study and work, we can gain a good
life with a purpose in mind.
Success and respect for ourselves will
come and we can better endure.

LET'S TAME OUR TONGUES

Although the tongue is small,
In our body, it is an influential part.
When we learn to tame our tongues,
We are off to a very good start.

We might use our tongue to manipulate;
Other times, we might complain.
We might brag, flatter, gossip or lie.
From these actions we should refrain.

Critical remarks can be hurtful—
Especially when we put other people down.
Nothing good comes from our wrongful use of words.
Let's speak with kindness and with a smile instead of a frown.

CALLING NINE-ONE-ONE

Every man, woman and child
Needs to learn when and how to dial 9-1-1.
Whether it's a wireless or a cordless phone,
There are things to do and not do, before your call has begun.

First, reserve the call to 9-1-1
Only for emergency use.
Stay on the line until you're told
The dispatcher is taking care of the on-going
crime, accident or abuse.

Whenever you call 9-1-1, listen to the dispatcher.
Tell where you are and what is going on;
Explain what the emergency might be;
And describe in detail what is wrong.

If the dispatcher tells you to stay on the line,
It is that she or he wants you to stay in touch.
The dispatcher is there to assist you—
His or her calm voice and assurance help so much.

WHY READ THE NEWSPAPER

If we read the newspaper and watch the news,
We'll see history come to life.
We can converse with friends and family
The determining issues of success or strife.
We need to be well-informed
Before election day.
We need to study the candidates and varying points of view;
Then at the polls we can intelligently have our say.
We might be interested to know about
Who is marrying or who has died.
We may want to know which team won in sports.
For which activities or meetings to attend, the
paper serves as a guide.
There are sections in the newspaper
Which tell of stock markets, entertainment and what's on T-V.
On certain days, there may be a special feature
And commentaries on what we can agree or disagree.
The newspaper has crossword puzzles
To improve our vocabulary and usage of words.
There are editorials and letters whereby people can speak out.
There are articles about state and national
parks, churches, animals and birds.

Advice is given in the newspaper,
As are the temperatures and weather reports.
We'll find the news of those who've been placed in jail—
All about their trials and the justice found in our Courts.
According to our varied interests,
There are book reviews that will entice and guide.
They can whet our appetites for reading—
The available stories which can reach us far and wide.

Current events can help us to become better citizens.
We need to be well-informed to decide about many things.
Let's not be ignorant about what's going on in the world.
Achieving satisfaction, a well-studied vote brings.

HAVE A PURPOSE AND A PLAN

It matters not if we're Hispanic, Black,
Yellow, Christian, Muslim or Jew,
One should not ridicule or make fun of me or you.

We cannot help who our parents are,
Or if we are American or born afar.

We should respect each other with love and care,
Because in this world we have the need to share.

We need to be friendly, if we want to have friends;
But seek those with whom our life style blends.

We have been given a chance to choose a
vocation or a professional career.
It is up to each one to choose wisely with wisdom, not fear.

We are given the opportunity to choose between right and wrong.
We are given the occasion to vote and make our country strong.

Now if there are those who do tease us or try to make fun,
It is best to ignore or report them, and they'll soon be on the run.

As much as is possible, we should live in peace;
Be kind to one another and let bullying toward others forever cease.

If we are true to our God, ourselves and our fellow man,
We can be happy and find a purpose for life and a plan.

BE FRUGAL IN
YOUR SHOPPING HABITS

Since many American's frugal habits have gone astray,
You need to be reminded to spend frugally yourself each day.
Don't be ashamed to wear your nice clothing more than once.
If they are classics, good and clean,
wear them—even for months.

Your spending habits will affect your budget and income.
Stay focused, cautious and practical until your shopping is done.
If you want a big item, try the layaway plan, rather than a credit card.
Buy store brand products; go to Goodwill, a
consignment shop, or a sale in someone's yard.

When you go shopping, buy only what you need,
So make a list of what you'll be shopping for, before you proceed.
Closets need not be filled with clothes bought in advance or
pantries filled with weeks' worth of food.
When you're not heavy in debt, you can
enjoy a happier life and mood.

If there is a Recession or a Depression that has come your way,
You can work, plan, and be responsible as a good steward each day.
Then live and be frugal with what you want and need.
Study, learn, save and good consumer instructions heed.

The poem above was inspired by an Associated Press article in *The
Gainesville Sun,* Sunday, November 7, 2010. The headlines were
"Americans' frugal habits here to stay." "Great Recession changed
consumers' approach to spending their money."

IT'S UP TO YOU

If you're not as pretty or handsome as you'd like to be,
It's the beauty inside that your God and others love and see.
If you can't walk or talk as you'd like to do,
It's the light in your heart and eyes that rings so true.

It's up to you, as others you meet and greet,
Look them in the eyes as they speak; hold your head high; let
your smile be sweet.
Put out your hand for a warm handshake.
You could be appreciated for your sincerity
and the stability of your give and take.

Listen to what others have to say.
Respond by writing, with your hands and your eyes, or with
your speech in some way.
A gracious "How do you do?" is a good way to start.
Begin a conversation, about a TV program, the news, movies,
books computers, or the best model of car or mobile cart.

There are jobs to train you for life's work.
Seek counsel, volunteer— your duties never shirk.
Always be on time; don't make others have to wait.
Stay off of drugs and alcohol; let your paths be straight.

Learn the policies and rules of whatever you try to do:
And to your God, yourself, and others, always be true.
Remember, you have been placed on Earth with a purpose in mind.
Be happy as you go about seeking— until that purpose you find.

BE A SUCCESS STORY

There are boys and girls between twelve and eighteen
Who go to bed hungry and crying themselves to sleep.
There are those who skip school and then find
They're in trouble at school and have even more cause to weep.

Some homes have a substance abuse problem.
Others have experienced domestic violence at home.
Still others are those who have been
psychologically or sexually abused.
With help they can become a role model and
no longer have to wander or roam.

If you are involved, talk with your counselors at
school, at home or with friends.
Rather than dropping out and getting into
trouble, turn your life around.
Even if you are an underachiever, have a family member in jail,
or are the product of a single family home,
Stay in school, study hard, participate in music and
sports and for success you may be bound.

There are counselors and mentors who have been where you are.
There are success stories of those who have been much like you.
Pay attention to these individuals who are there to help,
And success and happiness could come to you, too.

An article in *The Gainesville Sun* by Kimerly C. Moore, Staff Writer, Tuesday, November 2, 2010, was the column that inspired the above poem.

WHEN SOMEONE IS DIFFERENT

Just because we are healthy, handsome or
pretty and have a nice smile,
There are those who are hurting or may seem senile.
What do we do when we happen to see
Those who are different from us and not as happy as they could be?

There are those who have a congenital disease.
Can we by word or action put their hearts at ease?

If someone we know has a defect,
Do we try to help him or her, or do we ignore or reject?

If there are those who have difficulty with their speech
As they stutter or falter, do we listen carefully as they try to outreach?

If there is one whose body might be different from ours,
Do we stop and stare or treat them normally as our spirit empowers?

If someone we chance to greet
Has difficulty walking or moving his or her feet,
Do we offer help with the wheel-chair, wagon, stroller or cane?
Do we ever offer a shoulder or an arm to assist the lame?

If there is one in our class or group whose mind is "not all there,"
Do we laugh or make fun or let him or her know we care?

If we see someone who is blind and walks with a white cane,
Do we distract the seeing-eye-dog or a quiet demeanor maintain?

How do we treat those who have a different color of skin?
By being kind and respectful of each other are good places to begin.

We should remember that everyone has been
given a precious life to live.
Each one should be encouraged to worship, share and give.
Since there are those who are different in many ways,
Let us think of how we can help and find
ways we might give them praise.

NEVER SAY FAIL

We are told that "Half of success is a try."
Then don't be afraid and don't be shy.
If at first you don't succeed,
"Try, try again" by separating the flower from the weed.

We can learn each time we don't succeed.
It doesn't mean that we'll always fail.
It really means you dared to try.
Next time, you could have a "ship" that will sail.

To fail doesn't mean that you are inferior.
It just means that perfect, you'll never be.
It gives you reason to start over,
And with patience your goal can be attained, you'll see.

Failure does not mean that you are wrong.
Or that you wasted your time in what you tried to do.
It just means that you need to find a better way,
Start over! Your interests continue to pursue.

Never give up in what you really want to be or do.
Failure only means you have not succeeded yet.
If you had enough faith to experiment,
Then you've learned something, so have no regret.

GIVE A HELPING HAND

There are many children who are homeless
And are on the streets, hurting, hungry and scared.
They are looking for a way out—
Their lifestyles for which they're not prepared.

We can look out for these children
Who are sad, afraid and who are all alone.
Let's help guide and direct them to
A place that they might call sweet home.

There are homes for many children
Who need a place to stay.
Also, there are other mission houses
That are prepared to help children find a way.

If you are looking for a place to give a helping hand,
Sign up as a volunteer and give generously from your purse and heart.
You'll find that you'll be blessed
As service and gifts to others you impart.

A GUIDE—WAYS TO SUCCEED

IN APPRECIATION

A Guide—Ways to Succeed has been written in poetic form to encourage the children, youth, and others to read, explore and discuss the areas covered which relate to their everyday needs and problems. The hope is that more programs will be created to rescue youth from crime, as inspired by the **Alachua County Children's Committee** on **Rescuing and Keeping Youth from Crime,** Gainesville, Florida.

I am grateful for the many who have been involved in the project of the reinstated **Alachua Children's Committee** to **Rescue Youth and Keep Youth from Crime,** and thank those who have contributed to the cause. Some of those who have been involved and contributed much include:

Charles R. Page, while administrator of The North Florida Retirement Village, showed much interest and recognized the needs of the youth by sponsoring the program and later, after retirement, efficiently and graciously serving as emcee for the programs.

Mark Walker, the next administrator of The Village, was active in the workshops, sponsored and assisted with the meetings—reading, leading, and participating in the discussions.

Rick Heath, the succeeding Executive Director of The North Florida Retirement Village, showed interest in and support of the committee's work, but because of his short tenure, did not become very involved.

Mike Shimansky, Director of Dining Services at The Village and later Milton McGowian made arrangements for the meeting places and provided delicious refreshments, snacks and/or beverages.

Elaine Brown, Director of Activities at The Village, assisted in the scheduling of the meetings and making arrangements for available meeting places. She showed support by attending some of the programs.

Dr. Dan Boyd, Superintendent of Alachua County Schools, has been supportive, given talks during our meetings, and if he could not attend a meeting, has readily sent a member of his staff to participate.

Dr. Jackson Sasser, President, Santa Fe College, has given interesting talks and pledged his support in working with the committee and offered the possible parenting classes as needed. When not available to attend the meetings himself, he has graciously sent a representative.

Heather Jones, while an Assistant in the State Attorney's Office, and in her new position, is and has been a true and dedicated legal attorney who has participated in workshops, edited materials, helped with research, served in an advisory capacity, and participated as speaker for the programs.

Gretchen Howard, Director of Victim Services with the State Attorney's Office, joined Heather Jones in giving an outstanding presentation regarding the needs of children and youth.

Captain Tony Jones, retired from the Gainesville Police Department and is currently serving as Chief with the Gainesville Police Department. He has attended the meetings, given informational talks to the participants, offered advice, and assisted with having the youth at Reichert House complete surveys. In addition, he has attended the small group workshops and offered to read or have the poems read to certain young people on a trial basis. He continues his interest in the project.

Jean R. Craig Steel, before retirement from the Alachua County Schools, actively worked with children and teachers. She was an excellent source for sharing anecdotes, helping with current trends in education, serving in an advisory capacity, and registering participants for the meetings.

Dr. Fran Vandiver, Principal and Director, P. K. Yonge Developmental Research School, Gainesville, Florida, now retired, gave an outstanding talk to the Children's Committee participants. If she was not available to attend the meetings, she sent a representative. One of her talks inspired the writing of several poems.

Lieutenant David Lee, Juvenile Relations Bureau, Alachua County Sheriff's Department, participated as a speaker and shared some very interesting statistics and information.

Dr. Charles Hall, represented Dr. Dan Boyd, Superintendent, and as Director of Title 1, was a speaker at a general meeting regarding programs and efforts being made in the Alachua County School system. In addition, he was very supportive and attended large and small workshops by offering good information and counsel in editing the material.

Members of the school staff in Marian County attended a meeting and shared helpful information regarding what they were doing about truancy and absenteeism in their county. Matthew Lane, Director of Psychological/Social Work Services and Terry McCray, Lead Social Worker, Marion County Public Schools, presented an informative "Marion County Truancy Continuum."

Norma Hoffman, retired business education teacher, attended some of the meetings, made some sound suggestions, and even offered to teach the youth who needed and were interested in learning business skills.

Dr. Barbara Henry, Principal of Prairie View Academy and later Idlywild Elementary School, attended meetings and workshops and made good suggestions as to the needs of the children and youth.

Dr. Jo Ann Parham, Missionary to Africa, teacher of second graders, and dean and professor of education at Dallas Baptist College, has published a number of articles. She has been an active participant, has presented useful ideas, and assisted with oral reading and editing the contents of this book.

Former Chief of Police of Gainesville, Atkins Warren, now deceased, was very supportive, attended meetings, offered good suggestions, helped to edit the contents of this guide in small workshops, and continued to spread a good word about this guide.

Among others who participated and/or attended meetings included: Dr. Elizabeth (Buffy) Bondy, Professor in School of Teaching and Learning, U. of F., (Dean Catherine Eminovich's represntative, College of Education); Ginger Childs, member, Alachua County School Board; Tina Pinkoson, Alachua County School Board member, Alachua County Schools; Dr. Leanetta McNealy, Principal, Duval Elementary School; Dr. Robert Craig, Principal, Glenn Springs Elementary School; Lieutenant Daryl Whitworth, School Resource Officer, Alachua County Sheriff's Officer; Guy York, Vice-President of Santa Fe College, representing President Dr. Jackson Sasser, Myra Morgan, President, Altrusa International Club of Gainesville and Associate Director, Student Services, J. Wayne Reitz Union, University of Florida; Bill Baxter, Family Services and Altrusa Club,; Mary and Alvin Butler, Pleasant Street Baptist Church and Historical Committee Work; Rutha Harrison, Action Networking; J. C. Henderson, retired Judge and Village resident; Ruth Highberger, retired educator and Village resident, deceased; Louis Kalivoda, Coordinator for Police Training, EMT, etc., Santa Fe College; Lisa London, interested citizen, Pastor Steve Matchett, formerly with Action Networking; Rick Parker, Public Defense; Lee Pinkoson, County Commissioner; Paula DeLaney, County Commissioner; Harriet Spangler, retired teacher and former President of Alachua County Retired Educators Association, Inc.; Nancy Spiegel, interested citizen; Molly Springfield, University Trinity Methodist Church and Village resident, deceased; Jim Stringfellow, Success by Six; Mark Williams, Children's Services; Ester Tibbs, member, Altrusa International Club of Gainesville member and Family Services; Kris Williams, formerly representative for Dr. Jackson Sasser, President, Santa Fe College and member of Altrusa Club; Rosa B. Williams, Black on Black Task Force; Bill and Vickie Davenport, teachers, Gainesville Parent Project; Jim Lang, formerly Attorney, Alachua County Schools; Christy Cain, the Victim Advocate's Office, and Rebecca Mickholtzick, Assistant State Attorney, Juvenile Division Chief, participated in our small workshops and provided updates on services available.

Megan Rolland, *The Gainesville Sun,* wrote an outstanding article about the work of the Children's Committee and attended some of the meetings.

Irving Rill, financial banker, deceased, attended the general meetings and, after hearing the speakers, became an interested participant in the committee work.

Dr. Stanley E. Rosenberger, my brother, listened to and read some of the poems and made suggestions for clearer and more accurate descriptions. He has been a good source of counsel, encouragement and information.

Jerry Douglas, was Supervisor of Discipline, Alachua County Schools, assisted in an interesting presentation regarding discipline and attendance.

The Reverend John A. Parker, former Director of Missions, Santa Fe River Baptist Association and Baptist minister, has participated in almost all of the meetings and workshops since the inception and restoration of the Children's Committee. He is a good source of information, guidance, suggestions and advice. He has been faithful in attending the small workshops where reading and editing have taken place.

Eugene (Gene) B. Porter, friend of many years and a retired business man, understands and has observed first hand the wayward problems of children and youth. He has patiently read and re-read some of the poems contained in this book, and he made good editorial suggestions to make several poems more acceptable for use in the public school system and other institutions.

Joseph Ragosta, Dining Services Manager, Tower Club, North Florida Retirement Village, and then Milton McGowian have been very helpful in scheduling small committee meetings and arranging for setting up the work tables, furnishing cold water and delicious snacks for our pleasure. Evelyn McGowian and Chuck Dincher, Village dining services, assisted with this project by having snacks in place in comfortable work places.

The A. B. C. television programs on Saturday mornings, "Teen Kids News," provided updates, interests and concerns of children and youth that inspired some of the poems in this book. (Everyone, including adults, could gain much, if they ever viewed these 7:30 A. M. shows that were offered at one time).

Frances B. Head, wife, mother, English teacher, journalist and friend has shown her interest, understanding, skills in editing and clarifying the ideas of the poems in this book Her genuine love and concern for children and youth, support for the meetings and for this work have been an added inspiration. She has offered much encouragement and motivation, hoping that this edition will become **A Guide—Ways to Succeed** for our Youth.

Colleen Kay, Manager, Renaissance Printing, is thanked for her patience and all the skill and help that she gives in designing and laying out the work in a professional format for publication. Her work is appreciated very much.

Anne Heymen, journalist and writer for *The St. Augustine Record,* wrote a beautiful article about **A Guide—Ways to Succeed** for the local newspaper. Her interest in the poems and the article she wrote were graciously received. Anne has served as a successful journalist in St. Augustine for a number of years, and her article was shared with many interested individuals.

My thanks go to each and everyone for the part played in making this work possible and for those listed, those not known, and for his or her interest in **Rescuing and Keeping Youth from Crime.**

— *Margaret A. Rosenberger*

NOTES OR COMMENTS

A PROSPECTUS FOR A SCHOOL AND A POTENTIAL CURRICULUM DESIGNED TO RESCUE YOUTH FROM CRIME

Please complete and hand this form in before you leave the meeting. Circle or check the item with which you agree. In addition to English, speech, reading, writing, Math, and science there are other courses, subjects or tools needed in <u>preparation for life</u> which should be included in high school prior to graduation:

1. Bookkeeping skills to include ways to prepare a budget.   Agree Disagree Not Sure

2. Skills to deposit funds in the bank, withdraw funds, write checks, reconciling and balancing check books.   Agree Disagree Not Sure

3. Comparison shopping in stores.   Agree Disagree Not Sure

4. Instruction for building a house.   Agree Disagree Not Sure

5. Basic repair work on plumbing and construction.   Agree Disagree Not Sure

6. Sewing, darning, patching, washing and ironing clothing.   Agree Disagree Not Sure

7. Administering first aid.   Agree Disagree Not Sure

8. Ways to care for a sick person.   Agree Disagree Not Sure

9. Practical ability to bathe, walk or assist a person who is ill or has a broken bone.   Agree Disagree Not Sure

10. Administration of the Heimlich maneuver and CPR. (Cardiopulmonary resuscitation)   Agree Disagree Not Sure

11. Basics in cooking, setting a table; and the etiquette of good table manners.   Agree Disagree Not Sure

12. Acceptance of counseling, participating in role modeling, and reasoning together and learning to avoid rage, violence and hate crimes.   Agree Disagree Not Sure

13. Typing on the computer or typewriter.   Agree Disagree Not Sure

14. Responsible use of the Internet for research and information. Agree Disagree Not Sure

15. Study of and field trips to the correction institutions; such as, the juvenile detention center, city and county jails, Raiford, and other places of incarceration. Agree Disagree Not Sure

16. Study of ways to avoid going to jail: role playing and court trial simulations with judges. Agree Disagree Not Sure.

17. Visits to the homeless and study of the reasons for homelessness and consideration of the means of helping the homeless—other than providing food and shelter. Agree Disagree Not Sure

    A. Volunteering to help. Agree Disagree Not Sure

18. Basics of creative art. Agree Disagree Not Sure

19. Use of folk songs, patriotic songs and other music that can be sung together in a group or family setting. Agree Disagree Not Sure

20. Sports- exercise; participation, familiarity with rules and regulations. Agree Disagree Not Sure

21. Expansion of programs in the recreation centers to include the teaching of trades or crafts (for high school & older). Agree Disagree Not Sure

22. Training in the dangers and harmful effects of drugs, tobacco and alcohol. Agree Disagree Not Sure

23 Importance of good nutrition and nourishing snacks. Agree Disagree Not Sure

24. A course section on ethical behavior. Agree Disagree Not Sure

25. Acquiring a vocational skill or trade to enable each pupil to make a living for him or herself, should the need occur Agree Disagree Not Sure

26. Learning the basics of speaking Spanish. Agree Disagree Not Sure

27. Comparative religions and the significance of Christmas and of other legal or religious holidays and celebrations. Agree Disagree Not Sure

28. The return of sixth grades to the elementary schools. Agree Disagree Not Sure

29. I believe that the subjects listed above will inspire more productive lives than four courses in math for all pupils. (College will offer additional math., if needed.) Agree Disagree Not Sure

30. Acquiring parenting skills; keeping current with activities, and keeping in touch with school and P.T.A. Agree Disagree Not Sure

*******COMMITTEE WORK*******

A. Do you have suggestions for speakers? If so, list. Yes No

B. Would you like to volunteer to work with this committee or with school? If so, please list what you would like to do. Yes No

C. Others who, in your opinion, should be invited to our meetings or at school are as follows:

D. Comments:

Name_____

Address_____

Phone Number:_____E-mail Address:_____

Organization:

This form was prepared by Margaret A. Rosenberger, Gainesville, Florida.

CONSIDER PROGRAMS OF INTEREST AT AN EARLY AGE

The information below has been taken from advertisements received from Stratford Career Institute and other educational groups. The list might give youth suggestions of possible vocational program opportunities or interests. It s never to soon to start thinking, considering and exploring career advantages.

Accounting
Administrative Assistant/Secretary
Attorney
Auto Mechanics
Bookkeeping
Business Management
Child Day Care Management
Child Psychology
Creative Writing
Computer Programming
Computer Training
Contractor/Construction
Management
Cooking & Catering
Conservation/Environmental
    Sciences
Cosmetology/Esthetics
Creative Writing
Criminal Justice
Dental Assistant
Desktop Publishing Design
Drafting with AutoCAD
Drug & Alcohol Counseling
Early Childhood Education
Electrician
English as a Second Language
Fashion Merchandising & Design
Fitness and Nutrition
Florist/Floral Design
Forensic Science
Funeral Service Education
Gardening/Landscaping

Hair/Grooming Specialist
Home Inspector
Hotel & Restaurant Management
Internet Specialist
Interior Decorating
Locksmith
Medical Billing
Specialist Medical
Office Assistant
Medical Transcriptionist
Motorcycle Repair
Natural Health Consultant Nurse
Nursing Assistant
Paralegal/Legal
Assistant PC Repair
Pharmacy Assistant
Photography
Physical Therapy
Aide Physician
Plumbing
Private Investigator
Psychology/Social
Work Publishing
Real Estate
Appraiser
Relaxation
Therapist
Security/Police
Sciences Sewing & Dressmaking
Small Engine
Repair Space
Walks

Start Your Own Business
Teacher
Teacher Aide
Travel & Tourism
University Professor
Veterinary Assistant
Video Game Design
Wedding Consultant
Writing Stories for Children